DATE			

Finding Mr. Write

Finding Mr. Write

A NEW SLANT ON SELECTING

THE PERFECT MATE

Beverley East

VILLARD · NEW YORK

Copyright © 2000 by Beverley East
Foreword copyright © 2000 by Colin Channer

Library of Congress Cataloging-in-Publication Data

East, Beverley.
Finding Mr. Write: a new slant on selecting
the perfect mate / Beverley East.
p.   cm.
ISBN 0-375-50370-6
1. Mate selection. 2. Graphology. I. Title.
HQ801.E27 2000
646.7 7—dc21   99-048780

Printed in the United States of America on acid-free paper
Random House website address: www.atrandom.com
24689753
First Edition

Book design by Jo Anne Metsch

This book is dedicated to the first man who loved me,
my father, Mr. Aaron Alexander East (Brother Bertie);
my two heartbeats, David and Diag Davenport;
and my mother, Mrs. Winniebell East,
who gave me life, love, and courage.

Anything is possible, if you have faith.

—MARK 9:23

Foreword by Colin Channer

SCIENTISTS MAY DISAGREE, but I know this to be
true: Love is a basic human need, like shelter, clothes, and
food. By love, of course, I mean true love . . . love as reliable
as a sonnet, that strengthens your will like an anthem, that
stretches your mind like a novel, that calms your spirit like a
psalm. We know this love. It's the love that Jacob shared with
Rachel, that George shared with Gracie, that John shared
with Yoko, that Malcolm shared with Betty.

In a recent conversation on a flight to Ocho Rios, my
friend Alice, the world's greatest pessimist, described this kind
of love as rare. The plane was small—a turboprop with four-
teen seats. Her window framed the mountains. Mine looked
onto the sea, where the rising sun was ripening like an orange. "Is that kind of love as rare as the beauty of this sun-
rise?" I asked. She leaned away from her window and ducked
down, watching the sun rising through mine, and said in awe,
"Yeah . . . wow . . . I've never seen anything like this before."

To this I replied: "Could it be because you're looking through the opposite window?"

To open this book is to open a window and witness the dawn of a whole new way of finding true love—graphology. Simply put, graphology is the science of handwriting. Every person draws his letters differently, in ways both subtle and obvious, and so written words hold meanings that are deeper than the listings in a dictionary. You get to know a person not only by his words, but also by the way in which he writes them.

It is absolutely true—you can tell a lot about a man by his stroke. Is he faithful? Is he generous? Is he too attached to his mother? Is he domineering? Is he a coward? Is he sensual? Is he spiritual? Is he smart? Does he really like children? Does he really know how to, well . . . er . . . stroke it?

Written in clear, easy language, and ripe to readiness with hints and tips, *Finding Mr. Write* is a stimulating companion for anyone whose quest to find true love has been repetitive, boring, disappointing, treacherous, predictable, or bland. As wise as an aunt, as honest as a sister-friend, *Finding Mr. Write* is more than a book. It is an ode to truth, a praise-song for progress, a eulogy for players. Amen.

Contents

Introduction

WHILE A LARGE part of my work as a graphologist consists of consulting with professionals seeking to enhance their personal growth, as well as corporations, by far the most common inquiries I receive concern the area of relationships. The scenario is almost always the same.

After a speaking engagement or seminar on handwriting analysis, women rush up to me and thrust small pieces of paper into my hand. With a great sense of urgency in their voices, they invariably ask, "What can you tell me about this man?"—usually requesting information about a partner or potential partner, a spouse or their latest beau.

I decline such requests, first because the writing sample is usually insufficient (e.g., a name scribbled with a phone number, or a postcard message), and second because the owner of the sample deserves some level of privacy.

While I cannot ethically conduct such instant analyses during my public appearances, there is clearly a need to address the growing interest in handwriting and relationships. There have been many books written for the lovelorn, and now graphology may well be poised to become the millennium-era determinant of compatibility and those factors that serve as valuable indicators of the success or failure of a relationship.

Of course, there are numerous books in print on the fascinating subject of graphology, so I never thought there was a need for another. This book, however, invites you to look at simple characteristics of handwriting that can identify what makes your partner tick. It can help you cut to the chase and get to the point. The answers to your questions are in your partner's most powerful organ—his brain. Why? Because *handwriting is brain writing.* Everything you need to know about your partner is in his pen strokes. How he crosses his *t*'s and dots his *i*'s, his slant, his stroke, his pressure, and the size of his writing all reveal who he really is.

What makes *Finding Mr. Write* so different from a mere textbook approach, however, is that the book is based on my own personal testimony of what has worked well for me over the past thirteen years both within my relationship and as a practicing graphologist. I wanted to share this amazing and unique method with you. Having my husband analyzed was one of the best decisions I made in my life. (It's up there with having my son, and changing my career to become a graphologist.) It gave me a jump start into my relationship with him.

I had a lot of fun when I was single, but over the years, my single friends have constantly informed me of how the dating game has become a hassle rather than a joy. So I wanted to prepare this guide to assist those who have become jaded by the dating scene. It is written in simple, nontechnical language with easy-to-understand illustrations. Finally, I have combined this fascinating science with art in the form of poems, and anecdotes that may help you to remember some of the principles of graphology.

The book is divided into twelve hours of the day. As time is so crucial to all of us, I have given each area of interest a specific hour. There is no need to read the entire book (although I believe there is enough in each hour to capture your attention). Whatever you are searching for in your partner, just turn to the time of day that represents that characteristic. For example, if you are interested in his intellectual ability, turn to the eighth hour. If you are interested in what motivates him, turn to the seventh hour, and if you are interested in his sexual ability, race to the ninth hour—where you will also find the results of a survey in which more than five hundred men were interviewed to provide an informed view of what men really want from women.

I begin by addressing the number-one question: "Can I trust him?" In this hour there are handwriting samples of the good guys, the gay guys, and the sex offenders. If after reading this hour you find more than three negative characteristics in your partner's handwriting, you may consider not taking the relationship any further. There are even tips on how to bow out gracefully.

I then move on to the big picture—analyzing the presentation of the handwriting on the page (e.g., line spacing, margins). This reveals a whole image of his personality. Other hours of the day include a discussion of his ego, how he communicates, what his signature says, and how sociable he is. Answers to many of the burning questions you may wish to ask on your first date, but know you can't, can be discovered in these pages: Does he do drugs? Is he gay? Is he sensitive? Does he have a temper? There is also a quiz to help you prepare for your first handwriting profile—an introduction of yourself, through your own handwriting.

The eleventh hour celebrates those who have passed "the

seven-year itch." The couples in this hour represent a cross section of different backgrounds, ages, and orientations, including three gay couples. The longevity of their marriages/relationships spans from eight to sixty-four years—giving us hope that it can be done. If you are short on time, the quick-reference guide at the back can assist you in looking up individual letters. Later, you can turn to the pages that present more detail on the particular trait you are interested in.

The reader is encouraged to think about her own life purpose, through a self-testing exercise at the back of the book. It challenges her to realize what her needs are and to identify clearly the role she wants her partner to play in her life.

By the end of this book, you will have a better understanding of yourself and your partner. I hope it will assist you in making better choices in finding "Mr. Write." Personalities are complex and so are relationships, so don't expect this book to be a quick fix for all your problems. You will have to continue to work on yourself and your relationship. Remember that relationships are ongoing commitments. As we evolve and grow within ourselves, so will our relationships take different turns at different stages of our lives. This book invites you to consider seriously what you want for yourself and in your soul mate.

But first, we need to know what makes you tick. What are your strengths and weaknesses? What do you want in your ideal partner? Too often we are searching aimlessly. When you know who you are and what you want, the search becomes easier. Then you can go full speed ahead to find Mr. Write. The search does not have to be heart wrenching or time consuming.

A strong relationship can enhance productivity in our careers and in our personal lives. When we are happy in our personal lives we can benefit and prosper in our professional lives also, moving forward with pep in our step, a smile on our faces, and a new attitude in our hearts.

You do not want to spend too much time with the wrong person. You do not have the time to waste, especially if you are a fast-track career person or a student. No matter what your single status (recently divorced and just stepping out, widowed, or looking to marry for the first time), this book can help you to achieve more successful partnering.

Time is the essence of our lives. It's irreplaceable, it's enchanting, it's calculating, it's controlling. We can't eat it, feel it, or sense it. However, it does govern us from the very moment we enter the world. At any given time, your soul mate may appear and present himself to you. If you have any doubt when he comes along, he's not the one. If in doubt, leave him out. Meeting Mr. Write is all about timing and fate. We can't determine when he will appear. Although we often make plans such as attending a black-tie affair or a wedding ceremony in hopes that this may be the occasion when our potential partner may reveal himself, our expectations are often shattered.

Meeting Mr. Write is 60 percent timing and 40 percent fate. Usually when he comes, you are totally unprepared and looking like hell. The first time I spoke with my husband, it was 4 P.M. I was at work having a bad day and I was in a foul mood. Any other day, my secretary would have answered the phone to guard me from callers. This particular afternoon she was running an errand. The telephone rang and at the end of the line was a soft-spoken American voice remarking that my name had been given to him because I could help him find somewhere to live. I told him quite curtly that he had the wrong number. However, he kept me on the phone long enough to pique my interest.

Don't allow the mystic love of fairy tales like "Sleeping Beauty" or "Cinderella" to determine your life. You don't have to wait for your prince to come kiss you and awaken you to begin your life. Neither should you waste time with someone who doesn't love you, respect you, and appreciate you. When he comes, there won't be any doubt, no ifs or maybes. No matter how long you will have waited, it will have been worth it. Don't waste time worrying about the past—learn from it. You can't change the past, but you can invest in the future and what can be.

This book can change your approach to every piece of handwriting you receive. Every scribbled note, every birthday card, every Valentine, you will view differently. So while you're looking for the Hallmark sign, look at the strokes and slants of the script and signature, too. You will begin to read between the lines. You will discover so many hidden secrets.

So what are you waiting for? Take this journey with me to find out more about the stroke of a man. Your future is in your hands and can be "writefully" yours through analyzing your partner's penstrokes.

It worked for me. Enjoy the experience!

P.S. Although this book is geared toward men's handwriting, the same traits occur in women as well. There is no gender bias in graphology.

Finding Mr. Write

So Why Handwriting?

IF YOU WERE buying a house, you would get an inspector to look inside and out to check that everything is as it should be. Before buying a car, you would test-drive it. One of the most important decisions you will make in your life is choosing a partner. So *why* are we so haphazard about how we make this choice? We fall head over heels in love, and that is it. We are so blind in love that the partner we choose sometimes turns out to be the blind date from hell.

If you have been hurt in the past, you may spend so much time masking your true feelings that a lot goes unsaid. You may feel so vulnerable that you don't take enough time to get to know another person. You may trust too much too soon, or not trust at all. With little information you may jump to wrong conclusions. So why not try something different? Something that has been tried, tested, and proven. Something that is intimate and not intimidating. The more you know about yourself and the person with whom you want to be, the better the understanding can be between you. Many relationships fall apart from a lack of understanding. With all this information you can get a head start on your relationship and make better decisions for yourself.

HOW GRAPHOLOGY HAS HELPED
ME AND OTHERS

Judging from my own personal experience, I would suggest that a look at your partner's handwriting can provide a way to get to know him more quickly. Your partner may not be willing to acknowledge or even be aware of characteristics that explain why he does what he does.

When an analysis was being prepared for me, I asked the graphologist to look at my potential partner's nonnegotiable characteristics first (I did not know enough at the time to provide an accurate profile), those traits I knew I did not want to live with. Was he psychotic? Was he jealous? Did he have a temper? Was he deceitful? All of these were questions for which I wanted answers.

The graphologist returned with a positive response. No, he did not have any of the traits I suggested, but she gave me a long list of other characteristics and told me the type of man he was. Armed with that information, I was ready to understand my prospective partner better. The graphologist who analyzed him had never met him, but everything she told me thirteen years ago is exactly true.

I have been living with and working around the "other" traits, but I believe my graphological analysis gave me a jump on a fruitful relationship. We just celebrated our eleventh year of marriage!

TO BE FOREWARNED IS TO BE FOREARMED

I will start with the example of a bad-tempered man, my first experience in preparing an analysis for a couple. The young woman had requested it as a gift for her fiancé. They had become engaged a few months before I was asked to analyze them.

The man's handwriting expressed a great deal of repressed anger, plus a violent temper. I told the woman what I had seen. Her fiancé had a lot of glowing attributes but the level of temper shown in the handwriting was disturbing to me. She told me that I was right about everything else but was wrong about the temper aspect. "He is a puppy," she said, cooing. "We have been together five years and he has never raised his voice to me."

She wanted me to be present when she shared the information with him. However, everything did not quite go as intended. He threw the table up in the air and hit her in the face, breaking her nose. She had not asked him if she could do the handwriting analysis and he was angry that he had been found out. She later said I had saved her life. She would have married an abusive man and ended up as a battered wife. (The description of the temper tick is described in "Mr. Temper" on page 31.)

This was a horrible experience for me but I learned two valuable lessons:

1. Don't analyze couples without the consent of both parties. You could be opening a Pandora's box.
2. Don't make appointments with abusive people. I was lucky I wasn't hurt also. Watch out for the temper tick.

"THE PERFECT MATCH"

A few years ago a young man sent his handwriting to be analyzed for his career potential. His script was barely legible but from it I could determine an intelligent person with a great sense of humor and a lot of ambition. The more I studied the script, looking at each aspect of his personality, this man seemed a dream on paper.

I did not know what he looked like, but his profile for career and personality was very positive. I returned his analysis to him and requested he call me if he had any queries. He did not call but sent me a thank-you card confirming that "I was on the money." He had found the report helpful and, once he had his career on track, he would send me a sample of writing of the next woman he met. He said he had very little time to go out and meet women.

I also receive many requests from women for career analysis, and a few months later I did an analysis for a young woman requesting this service who, I realized, might be an ideal match for my career genius of a few months previous.

Although this is not part of the services I provide, I called the woman and told her what I felt. She was excited. I called him and relayed the same message. They received each other's phone number and promised to share profiles. Today, wherever they are in the world, they send me a postcard signed "The Perfect Match."

SO WHAT IS GRAPHOLOGY?

Graphology is not some New Age hocus-pocus, but the science of systematic analysis of handwriting according to strokes, slants, spacing, and pressure. Contrary to popular belief, it is not about magic, or fortune-telling or palm reading, or part of "the psychic network." It is a science validated by more than fifty years of work and research. Indeed, it is a highly structured discipline that dates back to the sixteenth century. Its guidelines have been developed and refined over centuries.

All the psychological sciences have long included body language as a useful index to personality. Handwriting may be the most revealing, however, since it provides insight into ability and aptitude. Handwriting is referred to as *frozen* body language, since any given sample of handwriting is unchangeable. It is essential to remember, however, that as we mature and grow, our handwriting changes. In this sense, handwriting is a moving and dynamic language indeed!

Every time you write, signals travel from your brain to your hand and then to the paper. The connection is so intimate that a few lines of handwriting provide rich material for analysis of the writer's personality, character attributes, and hidden potential. Handwriting analysis reveals much more than you realize about your emotions, what motivates you, even your sex drive. What handwriting analysis cannot do is predict your future. However, it can aid you in making better decisions for yourself.

In fact, the notion of graphology as an effective tool for personal analysis is often dismissed by the harshest skeptics as little more than an attempt to legitimize yet another psychic hotline—the type of scheme that must legally bear the disclaimer "For entertainment purposes only."

But this is not surprising. While handwriting analysis is widely accepted in detecting forgery or authenticating documents, the fact that it can be used more broadly to reveal intimate personality and character traits has not been well known—especially in the United States. My own introduction to the field is a case in point.

While living in London more that fifteen years ago, I applied for a position as a recruitment consultant. The employer asked that a handwritten cover letter be submitted with each applicant's résumé. After I was hired, I found myself working in an atmosphere that was almost unnaturally free of conflict—even though it was a high-pressure job.

My coworkers and I had such similar personalities that it occurred to me that we could well have been Stepford Wives—the cloned, perfect housewives of the 1975 movie. Was this just a fortuitous circumstance?

My curiosity compelled me to ask the owner just how she managed to assemble such a highly compatible staff. She immediately reminded me of the cover letter. "I knew just what I was looking for," she said. "I had no time to baby-sit personalities—so I had everyone's handwriting analyzed."

Equally shocked and intrigued by this revelation, I asked to see the report of my own writing. The in-depth accuracy of the analysis was amazing—it was definitely me. But how could a total stranger know so much about me just by looking at my handwriting? At that life-altering moment I became and remain a believer.

Immediately, I insisted upon meeting the handwriting analyst whose skills had affected me so profoundly. She was away lecturing in Paris at the time. But when we did connect, her quick perspective as an expert practitioner confirmed my decision to pursue the exciting field of graphology and explore its tremendous potential. Over the years, we developed a mentoring relationship that evolved into a business partnership.

The focus of handwriting analysis is constructive. It examines both the strengths and the weaknesses of a personality, but its goal is to help the one being analyzed to enhance what is already there and to facilitate changes that will bring out the best in him or her.

An in-depth analysis provides a clear and objective insight into every facet of your personality. It can be used as a working document for self-development. It gives us points to explore and enables us to discover our hidden talents and skills. It helps us recognize futile and dissatisfying careers as well as stagnant relationships. Our growing understanding of ourselves enhances our ability to communicate and interact with others. Often analysis shocks its clients with the quantity and quality of information it provides. The evolution of handwriting over time clearly indicates that growth can take place at our own pace and according to our own needs. It is important to remember that characteristics do not stand alone but must be considered as a group.

Apart from career and vocational counseling, relationship compatibility, and character development, handwriting analysis can alert you to potential health problems relating to stress and tension. It helps identify potential as well as direct talents. It can enrich our lives and give us the working material to become effective and wise.

THE PRINTED WORD

For the novice the easiest style of writing to analyze is the cursive style; the printed word will initially be more challenging, but the same rules apply as they do for cursive. Although you may not be able to identify as much as you can in cursive handwriting, you can identify pressure, size, and how the writing is arranged on the page. You can still identify your mate's or potential partner's goals by his *t*'s, how he processes information by his *m*'s and *n*'s, and his level of concentration and memory by the size.

The printed word expresses a fact-oriented person who is objective and unemotional. He will often shun emotional involvement and prefers simplicity and directness. Printers are often loners, aloof and critical within relationships. They are more independent and prefer to believe that they are in control of their emotions. They do not cope well in a chaotic environment. When there is a combination of writing and printing, there is evidence of unpredictability and emotional turmoil. There are several reasons why some people print:

- They do not know how or cannot remember how to write cursive, so printing becomes the easiest method for them.
- They prefer the visual appearance of print, or want to be understood with no risk of misinterpretation.
- If they are engineers or architects, the block form becomes a part of how they processes information, and becomes a part of their writing style also.
- They have had difficulty in learning to write and therefore choose to print because they are aware that their handwriting is illegible, or they realize that because of its form, printing provides a clearer message for the writer.
- The printed form creates an individualistic style for the writer. (Those who print may write totally differently in cursive. However, there will be some consistency in both samples, such as the height and the middle-zone letters. Only the slant may vary.) Printed handwriting, therefore, can be indicative of creativity, a visual, artistic expression.

FOREIGN LANGUAGES

For those non-English-speaking men who feel they can slip through the net: no chance. Foreign script can also be analyzed. Like the printed word, it may take longer and less can be identified, but as long as the sample is in roman letters there are clues that can be found. You may want to familiarize yourself with the alphabet of the given language first, because you will have to take into consideration the various formations of specific letters depending on the language. For example, the German alphabet includes a character representing two *s*'s, written like a *B* with a long stem. You would not be able to include this stroke as part of your profile. The German alphabet also adds an umlaut (two dots over certain vowels), another sign you would ignore. The French alphabet includes grave, acute, and circumflex accents over various vowels; these marks would also be ignored. With a full page of handwriting, other aspects of the writing can be considered: pressure, size, slant, and margins. These will provide enough clues to help you. You may, however, have to spend a little more time on this (German) sample.

WHAT IS NEEDED

A full page of handwriting is required to arrive at an accurate character analysis, for it is the overall picture that is important.

For the best results, you should request at least one page of spontaneous handwriting, done with an ink pen, pencil, or ballpoint pen, preferably on unlined paper. Felt-tipped pens hide such characteristics as pressure and decision making. Content is unimportant but the writer is asked not to copy text as this impedes the flow of writing.

Obtaining a sample may sometimes prove to be trying. Many people are self-conscious about their handwriting, even more so when having it analyzed. I suggest that you be open and honest. That is what you are expecting from your partner, so start the way you mean to continue. I cannot emphasize this enough. It can create animosity toward you and a lack of trust if you try to do this surreptitiously.

Tell your partner about the book; tell him you are eager to learn what makes him tick. Introduce some character traits of your own that you want to share with him. If you are willing to share he will follow your lead, but you will have to open the door. If he's not willing to provide a sample, don't push it. Leave it for a while, but watch out: What is he trying to hide? That will be a clue in itself. Try another time. Most men are open to trying new things. Find an aspect that may be of interest to him, but please respect his decision.

You may also want to purchase a magnifying glass. Inexpensive ones can be found in drugstores and at office suppliers. Such characteristics as deceit, self-criticism, and decisiveness are not so easy to detect with the naked eye, especially if the handwriting is small.

There are ten major aspects of his personality that we will be looking at throughout this book:

1. Integrity
2. Emotions

3. Fears and anxieties
4. Sociability
5. Ego
6. Communication style
7. Motivation
8. Mental processes
9. Energy and sex drive
10. Secrets in his signature

Each aspect will be explored with samples and illustrations.

FIRST THINGS FIRST

Before you begin thumbing through the book searching for clues in your partner's script, you must be prepared. Please do the following:

· Provide yourself with samples of your partner's handwriting and your own.
· Write down five things you want from your partner.
· List three things you don't want and then go directly to the hours that apply.
· Consider answering the complete self-test you will find at the back of the book (see p. 215–17) so you know exactly what you are about before you begin your search.

HOW DO YOU BEGIN?

You can approach analyzing a sample of handwriting in several ways:

- Quick glance—what is it that jumps out on the page first? Look it up with the quick-reference guide.
- Which characteristics are you most interested in? Go directly to the hour that describe them.
- The formal checklist approach, which most graphologists use (see checklist below).

CHECKLIST

Analysis is like putting a jigsaw puzzle together. Everything belongs in a specific place. When you are analyzing, be sure to search for the following:

1. Look at the *slant*—is he an introvert or an extrovert?
2. Look at the *t*'s—the *t*'s can tell you all about what motivates him.
3. Look at the *o*'s and *a*'s—what do they say about how he communicates?
4. Look at his personal pronoun, *I*—it will tell you his level of self-esteem.
5. Look at his *g*'s and *y*'s—they express his stamina, drive, and determination.

Each of the above will lead you to a picture of your partner.

So now you are ready to begin.

What could be the beginning of what looks and feels like a good thing could turn out to be disappointing. Remember, graphology is a tool to be used to enhance communication and to assist you in other ways. Be objective, and be careful how you use the information. You may find out information about yourself that you may not be ready to come to terms with, so think about your actions toward other people. I know when I discovered some things about myself from my profile—e.g., how I respond in a team environment, my level of concentration, my good memory—it took some adjusting on my part. Do not jump to conclusions. Look again, read, and pay attention to the clues in your own and his handwriting. Good luck in your search! Finding Mr. Write is easier than you think.

Integrity: Can I Trust Him?

I AM GOING to jump right in at the deep end, seeing that this is every woman's biggest concern. Can I trust him? Everyone is looking for a partner with the big *I:* Integrity. What we want is trust, sincerity, and a complete level of comfort with the person under consideration. For novices, integrity is the hardest characteristic in handwriting to identify, because combined characteristics can lead to wrong answers. So be careful. This is a trait you want to make sure you get right.

Never judge a book by its cover. Sometimes people are able to mask their vulnerability or their dark side for a long time. It is hard to detect many of these characteristics in a few dinner dates. It may take several months, even years, to recognize the true soul.

Sometimes when we meet someone he is showing us who he really is but we choose to ignore this. We believe and see only what we choose to, hoping that a perceived flaw will go away.

Trust begins with trusting yourself and being true to what you are. When you trust yourself, it is easier to trust your partner and others. Identifying integrity in handwriting involves a combination of traits. Some of the traits examined in handwriting analysis to determine a person's level of integrity are: dignity, loyalty, pride, sincerity, self-control. There are, of course, characteristics that will greatly reduce the level of a man's integrity: deceit, self-deceit, compulsive lying, and fear traits such as jealousy, temper, attention-seeking, dominance, low self-esteem, repression, and oversensitivity.

Here is what I call the troubled soul: Mr. Vulnerable. Sometimes a series of circumstances throughout a person's life can knock him off his perch, making him feel vulnerable. As a cover for his vulnerability, he may become defensive, exhibiting secretiveness and guarded behavior. He may be deceitful, oversensitive, resentful, or defiant.

Sometimes when these characteristics show themselves they are interpreted by others as malicious or insecure. We are all vulnerable to some extent, with unredeemable traits, but it is how we *control* these feelings that is important. How do we value the consequences of our actions? There is no such thing as a perfect person and we can be beautiful even with imperfections.

When these negative traits are found in handwriting, they are more than a flaw in character; they are signals for help, which sometimes go unnoticed until too late. However, you must remember that when you start a relationship with someone, you must accept him as he is or move on. Don't try to change him or think you are his counselor or his rescuer. Changes can come about only if he wants them and in his own time, not yours. You cannot change an adult. Even with good intentions on your part, he may resent you for your efforts. Hopefully you will love and value yourself enough not to venture down this path that will lead you nowhere.

In their consultations many of my clients have informed me that they have met someone who is wonderful and has many characteristics that they like. He is ambitious, he has good looks, a good job, money, and a nice car . . . *but* he has a temper, or he is abusive, or he has a drinking or drug problem. As uncaring as it may seem, I tell them that they cannot save him.

We start with deceit because a novice finds it difficult to determine its full meaning without evaluating all its characteristics. Deceit starts as a coping mechanism that allows us to avoid facing unpleasant realities and protects us from revealing our true selves to others. In time, this trait shows itself to involve many other traits beyond deceit. It is a very big red flag.

Mr. Deceitful

Deceit is revealed by **loops on both circles of the letters *a, d,* and *o.***

However, over the years I have interpreted this characteristic in different ways. For example, deceit in handwriting may not always signify malicious intent. An evaluation of other characteristics may determine other, related problems, or that the truth is being hidden to protect others. (A single mother of four may have to misrepresent the truth to get child support owed to her from her ex-husband.) Sometimes deceit is a warning signal of inner turmoil. It can be a protective measure, another way of hiding the truth about oneself as shown in the next example.

THE WRITING ON THE WALL

I once had a tenant in my house in London. In this young man's handwriting I found traits that showed deceit. My husband was surprised that I would consider a tenant with such a characteristic. I was confident that the rent would be paid, however, because it was not going to be paid by this individual but through the British college administration.

For over a year he lived in my house. The rent was paid promptly and he gave no trouble. However, nearer to the time of my return to the United States he became very agitated and restless, making many complaints about his apartment. On visiting him I noticed he had drawn a road map all over the wall. I commented that he had to clean the walls before his lease was up. I returned to the States and within weeks of my departure, the managing agent informed me that he had disappeared, leaving everything behind.

For several months he was missing. We notified both the police and his parents in Italy. He turned up in China. He was traced through his mother's credit cards. His parents informed us that he had a history of mental illness and that he had stopped taking his medication. He had been able to cover his disabilities for only a certain time. When the agent proceeded to clear the apartment for the next tenant, he realized the young man would have been found earlier if more attention had been paid to the writing on the kitchen wall. The map there revealed his plans for a fantasy journey—where he was going and how. Deceit in this instance showed itself as a cover-up of inner turmoil and a troubled mind. Deceit was combined with other traits in this instance: underestimation of self, intensity, irresponsibility, and stubbornness are telltale signs of a troubled soul. There should be a combination of two or more traits showing deceit to set off a warning signal.

1. Deceit was shown in the **loops on both sides of the letter *o*** in the words *you, from,* and *our.*
2. Underestimation of self was shown in the *t* **bars crossed low** in the words *East, note, that, current,* and *tenancy.*
3. The **size of his handwriting** was small and this intensified all his characteristics.
4. That he was fickle and irresponsible was shown by the **saucer-shaped *t* bar** in the words *that* and *tenancy.*
5. Stubbornness was shown in the *t*'s in *current, tenancy,* and *the.* The *t*'s **are crossed with a triangle on the left side of the stem.**

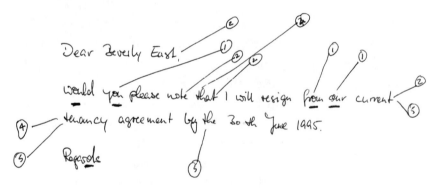

Mr. Self-Deceit

Self-deceit is indicated by the **loop on the left-hand side of the circle in the letters *a, o, d,* and *u.***

Self-deceit is a form of rationalization, when we make excuses rather than deal with real issues. Rather than accept the real reason for his doing something or take responsibility for his actions, the writer will find some excuse. The man in this case rationalizes his action because he does not want to own up to the real issue. He makes his situation more appealing to suit his own needs. He has become so comfortable in the security of his self-deceit that he no longer realizes how he is living. He is the Excuse King. No matter what he has done he has an excuse for it, and the consequences are never his fault.

Dad   I am not sure anymore

Mr. Compulsive Liar

Compulsive lying is indicated by the **figure eight inside the circle of the letters *o, a,* and *c*.** This stroke is very difficult to make and doesn't surface often, but when it does there is no mistake that it represents a compulsive liar. He cannot help himself. He may tell you a little white lie just to impress you. He tells so many that he no longer knows fact from fiction. Try to make this stroke yourself. It is not easy. So imagine how the writer's mind is working when he is making it.

o c a   good

Mr. Dominant

A tendency toward domination is shown in the *t* **bars pointing downward.** The stronger and thicker they are, the more dominant he will be. Do not become a statistic!

t   get to it right now

Mr. Abuser/Heavy Drinker

Substance abuse is indicated by the **detached letters,** although not enough research has been done to prove which drug has been used.

drug addicted men

Mr. Depressed

This man reveals himself by **downward sloping handwriting and heavy pressure** on the pen.

I hate my life

Mr. Sarcastic

This man reveals himself in script by a **sharp point at the end of the *t* bar,** hard to see with the naked eye. (The *t* bar doesn't need to be slanted downward.) The writer feels threatened by you and in defense tries to put you down with his bitter, caustic tongue—another no-win situation. The writer's insecurity could threaten his relationship with you.

Mr. Extravagant

This man reveals himself in handwriting by **large loops in the g's and y's.** He may shower you with gifts to get your attention.

gy

Mr. Stingy

His nature is shown by **tightness between words and letters.** He watches every penny he spends and watches yours too. If you are the extravagant type and like to live a high life, this man is not for you.

that's too expensive

Mr. Jealous

His handwriting expresses his nature by **small circles at the beginning of letters such as b, h, j, k, m, t, u, and y.** Look in the capital letters such as B, H, J, K, M, T, U, and W. The jealous man is insecure. His insecurity is fed by lack of self-esteem. His own level of self-worth does not allow him to believe he is worthy of your love and attention. He fears he may lose you, so he watches your every move and he doubts everything you tell him. These characteristics can drive even the most patient woman away.

Why didn't you take me?

Mr. Envy

He reveals himself by a **large circular loop at the beginning of *m*'s and *n*'s.** Envy is the sister to jealousy. No matter what you have or do, Mr. Envy wants to have it also or be
better at it than you are. If you are on a fast-track career,
watch out. He may try to railroad you or sabotage your en-
deavors to meet desires stemming from his own insecurities.

My Mother

Mr. Reserved

He has handwriting that **leans backward and is tightly
squeezed.** It looks like it could be written by a left-handed
person, but there is no such thing as right or left handwriting;
it is *brain* writing. The reserved man will be cautious and detached. He has issues from his past that will not allow him to
move as quickly as you do. He treads softly and cautiously
with you. He stays in a place of security, afraid of stepping out
to face the future and what it offers.

I am shy   *withdraw*

Mr. Repressed

He shows himself in writing by **squeezed letters,** which
causes him to **retrace downward letters** such as *h, r, m,* and
n. This gives these letters a cramped look. All his feelings are
pent up inside as a result of past experiences. Subconsciously
he is unaware that they even exist. (There is a difference between repression and suppression. Repression is an uncon-

scious defense mechanism that rejects unpleasant memories and emotions. Suppression is a conscious restraint.)

η mh   *my mother doesn't love me*

Mr. Abandoned/Rejected

He can be discovered when the **stroke of any letter is formed backward,** as in the case of *f*'s, *g*'s, *q*'s, and *y*'s.

Usually he has many unresolved issues that need to be addressed. Sometimes these issues stay unresolved for so long that he becomes comfortable with them and believes that everything is OK. Contributing traits that intensify this characteristic are the pressure of his handwriting and the slant.

f g q y

Mr. Attention-Seeker

In his case, you'll find that the **final endings of strokes come over on themselves** at the end of such letters as *a*'s and *e*'s, and that a **letter will join to the top of the next letter.** He is hard work, almost like having a child around you. He constantly wants praise and attention focused on him. He will create a setting so that he can maintain this drama. He is sick; he had an accident; he got fired. He wants you to tell him how wonderful he is all the time.

a e   more dates for me

Mr. Uptight / Tense

He reveals himself through **letters overlapping or tightly squeezed together** or **heavy pressure** that shows on the other side of the paper. Pressure, however, represents not only tension but issues stemming from deep-rooted experiences and emotions. When the letters are squeezed together, they often are a sign of poor communication, the inability to express needs.

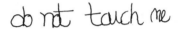

Mr. Idiosyncratic / Immature

He makes **circles over his *i*'s instead of a dot.** This habit is a trend among young adults who are searching for themselves and want to be different, who are distinguishing themselves from authority figures such as parents and teachers. However, when this trait is seen in the script of a mature person I am a little concerned about the man's level of maturity.

He wants to make a statement and stand out in a crowd: "Hey, look at me—I'm different." He will also want to have things done in a particular style or manner because he considers himself unique.

Mr. Stern

His handwriting has **very little bounce in the baseline.** An overall rigid appearance and a vertical or left slant is often found in the stern man's script. It is almost impossible to get this man to do anything spontaneous or to break out of his mold without much coercing.

My Way ɯ best

Mr. Pretentious

He puts **capital letters in the middle of a word.** He has very few real attributes but tries to give a false impression of himself to satisfy his ego. He is usually opinionated and self-righteous.

I like goiNg tO tHe oPera

Mr. Sensitive

He reveals himself by **loops in the *t*'s and *d*'s.** The larger the loops, the stronger the feelings of self-criticism. He cannot relax or feel comfortable around others because he is too busy worrying and concerning himself about what others are thinking about him. If you want to correct anything he says or does, you will have to proceed with great caution, always, of course, choosing the right time.

Mr. Possessive

His traits are expressed in the **hooks at the beginning of strokes.** He may not want to share you with others. If you are the social butterfly, this may cause some conflict. Check some of the other characteristics of Mr. Possessive to be sure that he is not a controlling, tyrannical, or dominating type of man. You could be in big trouble.

Why do you need more friends?

Mr. Impatient

Impatience in handwriting is expressed by the **bar of the *t* moving to the right and not touching the stem.** If the handwriting is vertical, this man may not be as impatient as the man whose handwriting slants to the right. Don't keep him waiting. He won't be happy, and neither will he wait if you are not ready.

t   I won't wait that late

Mr. Resentful

Resentment in the handwriting is revealed by a **stroke coming from below the baseline, leading into the upstroke of the letter.** This man will resent any invasion of his personal space and will not welcome unwanted advice. Tread lightly when you see him doing something wrong. He will not want you to advise him. He could be sensitive to criticism.

a   I don't want your advice

Mr. Fatalistic

When a **g, d, e, r,** or **y comes up in a loop and curls around at the top,** it indicates that this man is passive. His approach is fatalistic; his attitude is that, whatever happens—good, bad, or indifferent—"whatever will be will be."

Mr. Impractical

In the case of this man the *t* **bars will cross high and may not touch the vertical stems.** He is a visionary who sets high goals for himself but will not have the other, supporting characteristics to achieve his goals. He may be relying on you as a source of strength.

Mr. Impulsive

When his handwriting is **slanted greatly to the right** a minimum of 70 percent of the time and shows little control, caution, hesitation, or attention to detail, this is indicative of impulsiveness. The lines may often run off the paper on the right margin. This man is a loose cannon. He will run out and buy you a ring without asking whether you want to be married to him. His spontaneity can make him great to be with at times, but forethought and good decision-making ability will make him a safer life partner.

Mr. Selfish

A variety of traits can identify selfishness. The handwriting may be **slanted backward** and the letters may be **tightly squeezed with the final strokes ending abruptly,** showing no generosity. In addition, traits evident may be acquisitiveness, an **initial hook at the beginning of a letter,** or tenacity, a **hook at the end of a stroke.** This man will not want to let go of what he has acquired. He may want to be with you but may not want to share with you or change his lifestyle to accommodate your needs. He will always put himself first.

Mr. Defiant

This man's characteristic is expressed in his *k*'s. The **bigger the buckle in the *k*,** the more defiant he will be. He may make it large and out of all proportion to the rest of the writing. He doesn't want to be told what to do or how to do it.

k R   I am K ing

Mr. Narrow-Minded

This man's character is shown in his handwriting when the *e*'s **are closed.** He will not be open to new ideas or experimenting with new things. If he's used to sleeping on one side of the bed, that is where he will want to stay. New foods, places, and attitudes will not appeal to him. He will take a lot of persuasion and coaxing. If you want him to try some new dish—frog legs or snails—forget it.

e I dont need to try it

Mr. Perfection

He expresses his nature in handwriting when the **stroke swings upward and back over itself.** The *t*'s **may be crossed from right to left.** This stroke looks like a whip coming over one's back. Mr. Perfection is constantly whipping himself, never satisfied with what he has achieved or has done. He is always looking for improvement and perfection. He may expect the same from you. If you are happy with mediocrity, he may not be the one for you.

b let us try one more time

Mr. Temper

This man reveals his nature by a **small, angular stroke** at the beginning of a *t, h,* or any upward stroke. This angular stroke is not always recognizable by the naked eye. A magnifying glass may be necessary.

t Watch that temper tick

Thick, blotchy writing is often the first red flag. The sample below looks like it was written with a felt-tipped pen but it wasn't. **Hooks throughout the writing** and at the beginning and end of a stroke show a need to possess. The **forward right slant** expresses impulsive emotions. **Thick, strong *t* bar crosses** represent a strong-willed nature. His **overextension of letters** shows confusion and scattered energy. **Small margins** show his lack of respect for boundaries, both for himself and others.

> alled? Graphology. Funny, saw that Lewinsky handwriting analysis story in Time. Sounds like prison,———— suck favoritism. Sorry you & Mona are having trouble with thinness. I'm just the opposite. 'AT. Weighing around 190., 40 lbs. thinner than when I was on the streets. But still have a pot gut.

This man is serving time for murdering two people.

S A M P L E S   F R O M   A B U S I V E   M E N

The samples below show a disconnectedness in the script. However, this does not mean that men who print are potentially dangerous. Each sample shows the following:

· **Vertical handwriting** indicates the men are not emotionally charged but logical thinkers.
· Handwriting with a **straight baseline** indicates inflexibility.
· **T bars pointed downward** indicate a dominant and bossy personality.
· **Disconnected handwriting** shows a lack of connection with others.

IN ORDER TO HURT OTHERS

BEING CAUSTIC MAKES YOU APPEAR TOUGH, HARD, MACHO

I SHOULD TRY TO BE A LOT LESS CAUSTIC

BEING SENSITIVE MAKES YOU SEEM WEAK, VULNERABLE

THE purpose of Violence is to control of over power one

THE GAY MAN

I want to include the gay man here, because the integrity of those who are still not ready to come out is under question. A gay man may cause much heartache for the woman who loves him and is involved with him. Research shows that the following signs can be found in the handwriting of gay men:

A small circle at the end of the *y*'s and the *g*'s. This is indicative of clannishness.

y g

The falcon's claw—a hook on the end of *y*'s and *g*'s—is indicative of guilt. This is someone who holds on to guilty feelings.

Tension in the lower zone of letters *g* and *y* (can be identified only with a magnifying glass). A shaky line indicates actual tension within.

The signs indicative of secretiveness and self-deceit.

Although research has identified these traits, in my personal experience I have never observed these characteristics in the handwriting of gay men who are open and comfortable with their sexuality. However, in the case of men who are still unsure of themselves or not ready to reveal their true nature, I have seen some discord in the handwriting.

I would like those who read this information to remember that, like deceit, the interpretation of a "gay" trait is to be handled carefully. You could turn down a great guy, owing to graphology inexperience and quick judgment, simply because your interpretations of his handwriting lead you to believe he is gay. Other signs in his personality and his manner toward you will surface if you pay attention. Please remember that graphology is a tool to bring about better understanding between people and not a weapon to hurt, harm, or embarrass anyone.

HOW TO BOW OUT GRACEFULLY

If you find two or more of the negative characteristics previously mentioned in your partner's handwriting at this stage, you may want to excuse yourself from future dates. Already you are on the slippery slope downhill. There is no way to improve a relationship with a man who has too many negative traits without supportive and excellent professional help.

It is important always to be as honest as possible—although not so brutally honest that you don't spare any of his feelings. But the longer you delay a breakup, the harder it will be. Choose a time to tell him that he is not the one, or not the type of person you want to spend your time with. Don't go back on your word once you have made the announcement: another dinner date will not make it easier. If you really need help, give examples from this book of what you have discovered. Don't be disheartened; there may be a little wait, but there definitely will be another date awaiting you.

Now that you have examined the characteristics you don't want, here are samples of what the good guys' handwriting looks like.

A FEW GOOD MEN

Loyalty and sincerity are expressed by **clearly made dots over *i*'s and *j*'s.** These can be determined only by a magnifying glass. The lighter the dot, the stronger the loyalty. In order to build your picture of this man, you have to include how high his loops or strokes go upward in *t*'s, *l*'s, and *h*'s. His level of sincerity is reduced by evidence of any of the signs we have previously considered.

Here are some handwriting samples of a few good men.

Good Guy #1

· He is ruled by his head. His handwriting is mainly **vertical.**
· He is modest and often keeps a low profile, shown by the **size of the script** (small handwriting).
· He is direct and to the point. The *o*'s **and** *a*'s represent this.
· He is sincere. Look closely at how he **dots his *i*'s clear and clean.**
· A practical man, he **crosses his *t*'s halfway up the stem.**
· He is a fluid thinker, as expressed in his *t*'s **running through to connect with the** *h*'s.

Sorry for the delay, quick note as promised, Jean, Nzinga and Ndleh all send their love and are really happy about your successes. We look forward to a copy when it comes out.

Good Guy #2

· He welcomes distractions—the **large script** expresses this.
· He is ruled by his heart, expressed by the **forward slant** of his script.

- He is optimistic—his *t* **bars are crossed upward.**
- He has a lot of determination and drive, expressed in the **long *g* tail.**
- He is a good listener, expressed by his **open *e*'s.**
- His flexibility is shown by the **bounce in his script**—his lines are not even.

that it is, at least in part, due to the fact that it has been some time since I have trained. Like learning to ride a bike, I

Good Guy #3

- Simplicity is the key to this man, expressed in his **semi-print, semiscript** format.
- He is direct in his communication, expressed by **no initial strokes** to any of his letters.
- He is a sympathetic man, expressed by the **slight slant** of his script.
- He is a good listener, expressed by the **open *e*'s.**
- He is flexible, shown in the **bounce in the lines.**

Beverly has asked me to write several lines about myself. I am a recently married Legal Assistant, who loves his wife very much.

Good Guy #4

· He is a spiritual man, expressed in the **height of the *l*'s and *h*'s.**

· He is an optimist, expressed by the *t* **bars crossed upward.**

· He is a generous person, expressed by the **even spaces between each letter.**

· He is a warm, sympathetic person, expressed by the **right slant of his handwriting.**

[handwritten note:] Highest blessings for the upcoming book! I think you have a winner on your hands

Love,

All four men have similar qualities, and these are expressed in their balanced handwriting. All the zones that indicate a balanced personality are in place. Clear thinking is evidenced by even spacing between the lines. They are flexible, practical men. I am sorry, but all are spoken for.

Deciding which characteristics are important to you is a personal choice depending on your own values and standards. You can decide after reading this hour which traits you can live with and which you can live without. If your partner has too many of the negative traits, you may want to rethink your relationship with him. Remember to let him down easy.

At the Stroke of . . .

Three

Looking at the Big Picture

HANDWRITING IS AN expression of your very being. Just as your style of walk and talk represents who you are, so does handwriting reveal your personality. It gives a picture of you on paper, a snapshot of your personality. What you write is who you are.

When we are examining handwriting samples, we must consider a sample as a whole, because *no trait stands alone.* Each trait strengthens or weakens other characteristics within the sample. A total examination of a sample of handwriting would include the zones, baseline, pressure, margins, size, spacing, and slant. Every stroke that is placed on the paper should be a move toward the future. Strokes that steer themselves to the left or away from the future represent the past. The strokes that ascend represent the intellect and abstract concepts, or the higher being, and the strokes that descend represent the practical, social, and physical aspects of life. Let's take a look at each aspect:

ZONES

In handwriting analysis three zones of writing concern us. We refer to them as the abstract (the upper zone), the mundane (the middle zone), and the material (the lower zone). Each has a special significance to the analyst. The relationships were discovered and described by the Swiss psychologist Dr. Max Pulver. The diagram below will help you remember which zone belongs where.

You may think of the zones as you would a person's body. The upper zone represents the head, the mind, ethics, philosophical concepts, and morals. The middle zone represents the emotions and means of communication. The lower zone represents the legs, standing for energy, drive, and stamina.

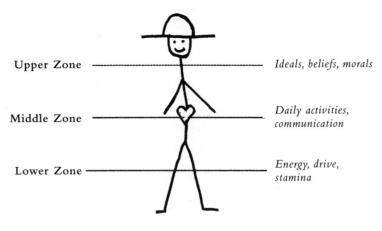

Upper Zone — — — — — — — — — — — — —   *Ideals, beliefs, morals*

Middle Zone ———————————   *Daily activities, communication*

Lower Zone ———————————   *Energy, drive, stamina*

Zones in words

UZ
MZ
LZ   *lovely long legs*

His Morals, Understanding, Ethics, Concepts

The upper-zone letters are those whose strokes extend upward. The **higher the stroke extends upward in comparison to the zone of the small or mundane letters,** the stronger the writer's degree of interest in abstract philosophical and spiritual matters. These letters are *b, d, f, h, k, l,* and *t.* The upper-zone letters will reflect the writer's ideas, beliefs, ethics, and standards. All three areas should be equally balanced. If the **upper-zone letters are much taller than the letters in the middle zone or if the middle-zone letters extend too high into the upper zone,** this reveals discord in the personality.

Upper Zone

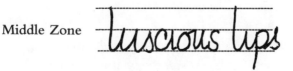

Heartbeat

The middle zone embraces all letters not projecting into either of the other zones. These letters are *a, c, e, i, m, n, o, r, s, u, v, w, x,* and *z.* They constitute the writer's heartbeat. They reflect day-to-day activities requiring little conscious effort. The middle-zone letters correspond to the part of the man that is sociable and accommodating, that lives mostly in the here and now and has very little concern for the future.

Middle Zone

Energy, Stamina, and Passion

Letters made by strokes descending into the lower zones *(g, j, p, q, y,* and *z)* stand for drive, energy, and stamina. The **longer the stems,** the stronger the drive and energy. **Size relative to the letters of the emotional zone** indicates degree of interest and endurance. (Note that the letter *f* falls in all three zones.)

Lower Zone *long legs*

Does the Writer Have His Feet on the Ground or His Head in the Sky?

The baseline is the imaginary line he creates in his writing when there are no ruled lines. If a man writes on ruled paper, the line already exists. The baseline he creates on unruled paper shows his level of reality and how flexible or inflexible he is. The **straighter the line** is when he writes a sentence, the more inflexible he is. The **more bounce in the script,** the more flexible and realistic the writer is. When the **writing hugs the ruled line,** this shows a sign of insecurity and inflexibility.

-------------------------------- Inflexible

Flexible

PRESSURE

The easiest way to check the pressure in handwriting is to turn the page over. If you can feel the writing on the back, almost like braille, the man is too tense or stressed out and has a whole lot on his mind. It may be advisable to help him relax before you overwhelm him with words of commitment.

Heavy pressure in handwriting can also indicate a person with troubled emotions from his past. How will he deal with life's dilemmas? Will he buckle under pressure or will he resist and fight back? The heavier the pressure, the greater the turmoil lurking within him. Depending on the **slant of the handwriting,** he could suddenly wake up one day and snap at someone for a minor incident. It is not that day's incident that is really bothering him but pent-up emotions—anger and hurt from past experiences. If his **handwriting is vertical,** his emotions are kept under a tighter rein of control.

Light pressure means emotions fade fast—the person forgives easily and does not hold on to experiences for a long time.

Light

Medium

heavy

SIZE

What is the significance of the size of handwriting? The size is the writer's projection of self-importance. Writing size usually indicates the size of the writer's claims among other people. It is a measure of his need for recognition and indicates his attention span.

Small Script

Contrary to common belief, small handwriting does not mean stinginess. However, the smaller the script, the higher the level of concentration and productivity the writer has. He will not want to waste mental energy but focuses on the task in hand. Small handwriting is a sign of superior concentration and intelligence. The writer is very detail-oriented. He will be more intense than one with larger script. Every characteristic of his personality will be intensified (e.g., if you meet a man who is stubborn, and his handwriting is small, he will be four times as stubborn as a man with larger script). The man with small script is more likely to screen his calls and doesn't welcome interruptions. Remember what you tell him: He also has a good memory.

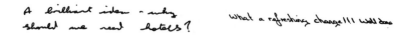

Large Script

Large handwriting expresses high awareness. Men with large script like to make an impression on everyone around them. They may enjoy attention and admiration. Their forceful personalities may gain them many admirers. These men need constant movement and activity because they find it very difficult to sit still for long. When they have to concentrate, it takes an effort of will. They welcome distractions readily. Call them anytime.

such a letdown when you look forward to a given situation and things do not work out in your favor. I can not afford to be ~~[crossed out]~~ optomistic, and credit this

SPACING

Intuition

Breaks between letters express a high level of intuitiveness. It is as if a sixth sense or inner voice guides the writer through life. In your relationship with such a man a lot can certainly go unsaid, because intuitively he will know when something is wrong with you. He will know which is the right stance to take in any given situation.

The amount of space between letters shows the extent to which he relies upon cooperation with others or on his own intuition. The size of the space is a nondeliberate act. As in each of the factors previously studied, be aware that letter-spacing supplies only one clue to the total picture of the writer and must be assessed along with other characteristics. You will find this consistently throughout the book. *No characteristic stands alone.*

I always go by my gut feeling

Give Him His Space

Spacing between words shows the degree of contact the writer establishes with his immediate environment. It is a reflection of his orderliness and his efficiency in use of time. If he shows wide spacing between words, he may not want you or others around him too often. So don't crowd him.

Below is the handwriting sample of a person who lived in total isolation for several years. You can almost put an additional word in each word space.

and for a long time I was glad to be on my own. Then I recovered! Last July I took the plunge and answered

Clarity or Confusion?

Even spaces between lines express clarity of thought in the writer's actions. The writer will be organized and a forward planner. This clear-thinking person has everything in place in his head.

jewelry; and a wide markets were certainly men and women in many Tibetans, who shaggy ponies clean

Watch out when **lines run into each other;** this expresses confusion. The writer often overwhelms and overextends himself. You will often get frustrated with a man of this type because he is usually running behind schedule. He often tries to squeeze in just one more appointment before you meet for dinner. If you are concerned about punctuality, this man may irritate you if he is always calling to tell you he is running late again or just turns up late.

MARGINS

The manner in which a man fills a blank sheet of paper represents his intellectual and emotional concepts of the world. How the writing is framed on the page is a reflection of how he perceives himself as functioning in his environment. How he utilizes the space on the paper shows how he sees himself in relation to the world. The margins formed on the paper express an unconscious frame for the space he occupies in his life. His emotional and psychological perspectives will determine where he is inclined to place the pen on the paper and start writing. He can see himself either as active in the world or passive, depending on how much of the paper he uses.

Does He Resent Authority?

If the writer starts very **close to the top of the page,** he is more of a forward thinker than a doer. He dislikes authority and lacks respect for it. He doesn't handle rules and regulations well. He will have a greater interest in the abstract world and things pertaining to it.

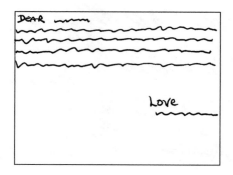

Does He Prefer Isolation?

When the **bottom margin is too large** and he completes his script two and a half inches or more from the bottom of the page, it indicates that he is too isolated and out of touch with reality and life.

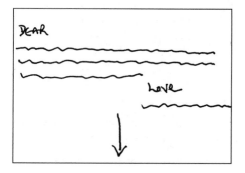

Is He Insecure?

When the **bottom margin is too small** and there is hardly any space at the bottom of the page, this shows that he is depressed and insecure.

Does He Respect Your Boundaries?

The right margin is less of a deliberate choice than the left margin. Only rarely do we see the right margin constructed evenly. As the writer moves across the page, the lines produced show his willingness to accept the future and people more readily. The right edge of the paper represents the future. The wider the right margin, the more reluctant the writer is to move ahead and create new events in his life.

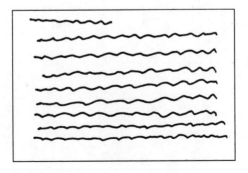

Is He Reluctant to Face the Future?

A **wider than normal right margin** shows a reluctance to approach the future.

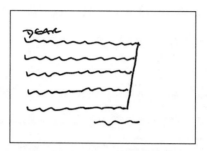

A **narrow right margin** shows self-assurance, spontaneity, and an attitude of expectancy toward life and the future. When the writing runs off the page he has no boundaries within his own life and therefore will not respect the limits of others.

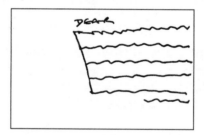

Does He Stay Close or Prefer to Escape?

At a very early age at school, our left margins were determined for us by the predrawn margins on our writing tablets. As the writer develops into an adult and begins to make decisions for himself, he will determine his own destiny.

The **closer he writes to the left edge** of the paper, the more he sticks to the past and images of security.

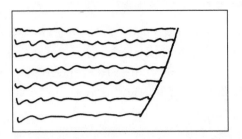

An **extremely wide left margin** can indicate a strong unconscious desire to escape from an unhappy past.

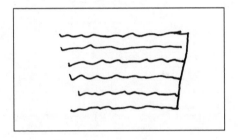

Is He Ready to Move On?

When the **left margin becomes progressively wider** at the end of the page, the writer is willing and eager to forget his past and move away from what has been and get on with his future. He gains confidence with each stroke and stride.

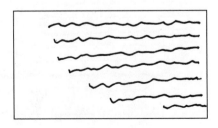

Does He Live in the Present?

When we encounter a page of writing on which **all four margins are abnormally wide,** we know we are dealing with a person who is unwilling to come to grips with reality. He may be aloof, socially withdrawn, and live most of the time in the present.

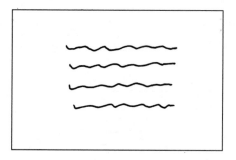

Is He an Organized Forward Planner?

Narrow margins all around indicate that the writer is usually very involved in his life, and because of his involvement he is usually organized and a forward planner. Check the line spacing for clarity. If the letters are overextended, then he pushes himself beyond his limits. He will most likely put many demands on you too.

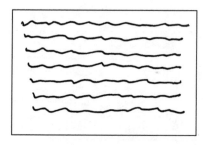

Is He Intrusive?

A man who **uses every bit of the paper and leaves no margins** is trying to get the most out of life. He has no limits. He may infringe on your privacy by turning up unannounced. He can be intrusive, so look for clues in how he communicates to determine whether he is sincerely in need or merely greedy.

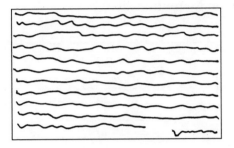

IS HE SOCIALLY AT EASE?

A **balanced margin on all four sides** of the page shows a man who is at ease socially and comfortable with life in general. He paces himself realistically and is usually quite well organized.

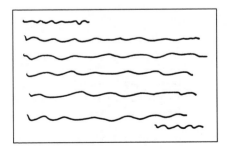

IS HE ALOOF AND UNSOCIABLE?

A **left margin that gets progressively narrower** as the writing progresses down the page shows the writer is gradually losing confidence and needs much reassurance to keep steady and on track. His enthusiasm wanes under pressure. He may be a little aloof and withdrawn at times. For other clues look for the spacing between words and the slant indicating how he responds emotionally.

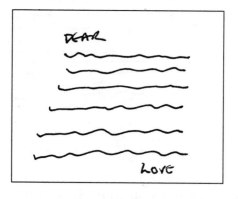

At the Stroke of . . .

Four

Sociability

In our kindergarten days we were taught to write on lines, and to create each letter between two horizontal lines (you remember—with the dotted line running between them?). We carefully followed the instructions of our beloved teachers. However, as we became adults and developed our own personalities, most of the forms and influences from the classroom took on an individual appearance. When we write on unruled paper, the line we create represents how firmly we have our feet on the ground (i.e., the baseline). The first step toward identifying our emotions is by measuring the baseline to identify our level of reality. The emotional makeup of an individual is the foundation on which the whole personality rests.

When bounce is evident in writing, it expresses flexibility and the ability to accept change. The writer's emotions are revealed by the way the handwriting slants. For an accurate picture, the slant of the handwriting is carefully measured by counting a continuous series of up strokes. However, for quick insight into your potential mate's emotions, here are some general examples of the slant:

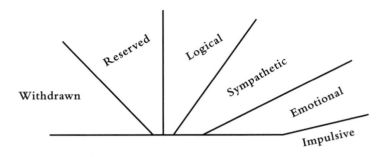

EMOTIONS

Mr. Extrovert

The slant of the handwriting expresses the writer's emotions. The farther the **handwriting slants to the right,** the more expressive and emotional he is. An extrovert ruled by his heart and not his head, he cannot conceal his feelings for long. He makes decisions based on his emotions. He will rarely take time to analyze or think things out. He will need constant feedback from you. His fears and anxieties are greatly intensified by his strong emotions, as indicated by the size of his script.

Mr. Introvert

The more the **handwriting slants to the left,** the more withdrawn and reserved the writer is. There will be issues from his past that he has not been able to solve or move forward from. He may be introverted to an extreme. He needs to be handled with kid gloves. (Your first reaction might be to assume that handwriting slanting this way comes from a left-handed writer. That is a misconception; left- or right-handedness is irrelevant in handwriting analysis. Remember, handwriting is a signal from the brain, so the hand one writes with is of little importance.) The writer can appear outgoing but does not reveal personal information.

Mr. Logical/Practical

The **more vertical** the handwriting, the more controlled the writer's feelings. This man is ruled by his head and not his heart. He is logical and practical. When he decides to take you on a date, he will be more practical and lack spontaneity because everything has to be planned in advance.

He thinks everything through carefully. He is likely to be sincere. In a crisis, you can depend on him to make decisions based on facts and not emotions. He is a hard person to get to know because so many of his true emotions are submerged. It will be hard to pull him into all your emotional crises.

Remember me!
Have a brilliant
Christmas and a
joyeux New Year
Much love

Mr. Moody / Temperamental

Handwriting that **goes in all directions within a word or a sentence** indicates changing emotions. In the same word the slant could change from one direction to another. You call the writer one day and he is ready to be with you and meet your every need. A week later you call him and he wants to be by himself and doesn't give much of an explanation. He is usually unpredictable. He normally does not understand himself, much less you. Look also at how he communicates. Is he the silent type? If he is a man of few words, there will be few or no explanations. His attitude is usually immature.

I am not moody at all

Although the following samples are not representative of the slant, they will be helpful in assisting you recognize other social skills.

Mr. Uninhibited

Handwriting that shows **wide letters** such as *h*'s and *b*'s and has a **right slant** expresses his ability to be spontaneous and open. He's an anything-goes kind of guy.

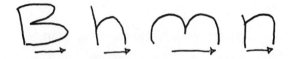

Mr. Loner

This man's handwriting will be marked by **long strokes with no loops in the *y*'s and *g*'s.** He is someone who enjoys his own company. He is not necessarily unsociable but needs time to be by himself. Please allow him his space. In a relationship it is important to recognize each other's needs as early as possible. You could lose someone simply because you are always trying to get him to be a part of various social activities when this is not what he wants. He would prefer to be alone or just spend some quiet time with you. Respect his needs. Doing so will take you a long way.

.l RESPONSibilit̶y̶ for̶ his or̶ her̶
state of health and well being.
State of mind involves taking
active role in adopting a
style that includes such

Mr. Selective

This man's characteristic is indicated by **slender loops in the *y*'s and the *g*'s.** Some men seem friendly and social on the surface, but deep down they are very selective about the company they keep. Only the chosen few will fit this man's small, handpicked circle of friends.

Mr. Clannish

The clannishness trait is expressed by **small circles at the end of the *y*'s and *g*'s.**

This man likes to be around people with characteristics and interests similar to his own. He will be attracted to you by your similarities. Rarely will he venture out of this mode, so don't be fooled into thinking that he will spread his wings much farther, even if you do at times. His level of insecurity has caused him to select and trust a certain clique, a group of people with whom he has a common bond.

Mr. Self-Conscious

This is revealed by a **final hump in the *m*'s and *n*'s that rises above the rest of the letter, or when the second of double letters is higher than the first.** You may be a social butterfly, at ease with everyone, anywhere, anytime, but Mr. Self-Conscious will feel that others are watching and judging his every move. This may not be the case, but it will be hard to convince him otherwise. If you are a social butterfly, you will have to break him in slowly and gently to your social circle.

Mr. Restless

Long loops in *p*'s, *f*'s, and *g*'s, and long *y* and *g* endings characterize this man.

The restless type needs to be on the move; he cannot keep still. He will not want to stay home in front of the TV. He may enjoy a great deal of outdoor activity and may want you to be a part of that life also, depending on other characteris-

tics such as ethics and loyalty or lack thereof. With his strong
need for variety and change, he may not want to be a one-
woman man.

Mr. Restless is a three-time marathon runner.

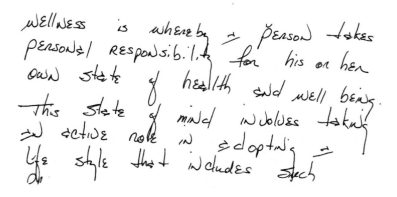

Mr. Nurturing

This man is revealed in the *a* **that has a cover on the top
of its stem.** He acts in a protective and nurturing manner.
Look also at how his handwriting slants. A slight slant indicates a sympathetic nature.

Mr. Pushover

This trait is expressed by the **roundedness of the *s* shape.**
No matter what is going on in his life, he may buckle under
pressure or back down in an argument. Check other traits
such as willpower and determination, which will help him
along when he is faced with obstacles.

Mr. Independent

The simplicity of these strokes suggests that no extras are needed in this man's life.

I Keep it simple

Mr. Shy/Reserved

When **any letter is thin and there is no room between the strokes,** it expresses a man with whom you may have a hard time being outgoing and sociable. He is exceptionally inhibited. You will have to handle him with care.

I'm a home body

Mr. Aloof

This trait is expressed by the **disconnection in the letter k.** Also look for large spacing between words (see page 46). If his handwriting is vertical, it may also add to this trait. He may not seem to be having a good time, especially in a public setting, but this man is often unsure how to express himself.

Ic K

Mr. Uncompromising

This man is revealed when his **downstroke pulls away from the stem in letters such as *d*'s and *y*'s.**

Mr. Empathy

This trait is expressed by **open *d*'s, along with a right-slanted script.**

An alternative method of identifying his sociability is by looking at the way his strokes are formed. The more **curved and rounded** a stroke is, or garland shaped, the more accommodating he will be to others. His handwriting emphasizes a lack of stress or friction in his personality.

The handwriting stroke that produces **angles** signifies the possibility of conflict. The writer is likely to be careful, methodical, and analytical.

The **arcade stroke** is the opposite of the garland form, since it is created by an upward curved or humped stroke. The writer gives a great deal of careful thinking and attention to form.

Thread writing, made up of **formless strokes,** suggests speed and impatience, since the letters are only barely recognizable.

At the Stroke of . . .

Five

The Ego:
The *I*'s Are the Window
to the Soul

THE EGO IS the *I* that resists and holds its ground from becoming *we.* The ego and the level of confidence of an individual are part of our birthright. One's ego can certainly play
havoc in a relationship. It is important that we understand this
aspect of the personality as quickly as possible. Our image of
self-worth is developed in the formative years of our lives.
The images of ourselves continue to be shaped and reshaped
and affect us as we develop and encounter various experiences along our life's journey.

However, depending on how we were nurtured by the
people that helped to shape us, we can either be greatly en-
hanced as individuals or deprived. The messages from our
parents, siblings, relatives, caregivers, and schoolteachers were
important to our development. Self-confidence is reinforced
with kudos, gifts, and an abundance of attention and care
when a child does the right thing. If a child is scolded and
criticized unfairly with harsh words, his self-image may suffer.
He may grow into a resentful and insecure individual. This

experience may affect his behavior in how he seeks approval from others.

As little girls, the first man we loved was our father, if he was present in our lives. The way your father nurtured you will have a profound effect on how you view and relate to other men. The relationship we developed with him in our formative years will greatly determine how we develop and form relationships with our partners in womanhood. Many women raised without a male figure in the house may seek attention from men in any form they can receive it, if their self-esteem is low. They may often be looking for the father figure they did not have as a child. If her father was cold and uncaring, a woman may have difficulty in trusting or being close to other men. If her father was kind and protective, however, her expectations of her partner may be the same.

If your father was harsh and disrespectful to your mother, it may be hard for you to trust any man. You may be harboring anger for the actions of other men—stepfather, uncle, or any other male in your life. For a man, how he saw his father interact with his mother may be a determining factor in how he will respect or interact with women.

The *I* (the personal pronoun *I*, not the capital *I*, which is attached to another letter) is the only stroke that will give us some indicators on how a man feels about and perceives himself. What is preferred to be seen in handwriting is a strong personal pronoun *I*. Too large an *I* can represent too much ego, vanity, or a false perception a man has of himself. How he writes his *I* will offer a valuable tool for assessing his private needs and values, in revealing aspects of his soul. It can also suggest harmonious or destructive elements within his life. This single letter can reveal the importance of the male and female authority figures of his experience and background and how his relationship with those models affects his relationship with you.

Our relationships with our parents can also be identified by this one letter. The ego reveals where we have come from, how we have allowed our experiences to shape us. We can change our lives as we evolve, but the *I* is the only stroke within this book that can be analyzed alone to give you a clear picture of your image and your prospective partner. The personal pronoun can take on any form. It can look like the copybook letters we learned in school or the various other scripts we have learned over the years. You should consider the size of the *I* in relation to the size of the rest of the writing and the signature.

The personal pronoun *I* offer clues to our total self-image. You can almost become your own private investigator.

Here are several *I*'s familiar to us:

the copybook *I*   the printed *I*   the cursive *I*

MATERNAL INFLUENCE

A mother's influence is shown when the **top of the *I* stem is longer than the bottom of the *I* stem.** It appears in any of the following, whether it is the printed *I* or the cursive *I*.

THE PATERNAL IMAGE

A father's influence is shown if the **bottom stroke of the I is longer or the loop is bigger.** Here is a sample of a young man who was raised by his father from the age of nine.

"I AM SELF-CONFIDENT"

This is indicated by a **large I,** no matter what form it takes, as long as it is balanced within the rest of the script.

"I LACK SELF-CONFIDENCE AND HAVE LITTLE SELF-WORTH"

This is indicated by a series of small *i*'s. When the **I is not a capital but a small *i*,** the writer indicates he feels worthless in the eyes of himself and others.

"I AM EGOTISTICAL AND HAVE AN EXAGGERATED SENSE OF MY OWN IMPORTANCE"

This is evidenced when the *I* is **written three times larger than the rest of the writing.**

"I AM DIGNIFIED"

Added to vanity, dignity is more pronounced. It is revealed by a **retraced *I*.** The writer is very conscious of his personal image and how others view him.

"I AM PROUD"

Pride is shown in the handwriting when the *I* is **two and a half times bigger than the rest of the script.** Pride is evidence that we feel good about what we do.

"I AM AN IDEALIST"

This is shown by a **large letter with a loop in the upper zone.** The idealist likes to deal with ideas or concepts and sees himself as beyond the ordinary.

"I AM INDEPENDENT"

A **straight-line *I*** represents simplicity and straightforward-ness, a person who is independent, clear, and concise. He needs to stay aloof and unencumbered by the demands of conventional life. Best way to please him: keep it simple.

"I AM TIMID"

This is evidenced when the ***I*** **has a retraced upper loop.**

"I AM AGGRESSIVE"

This is expressed by **angular strokes made with heavy pressure and rising from the baseline.**

ℓ am

"I HAVE A HARD TIME STICKING TO MY COMMITMENTS"

This is displayed by the **stroke's going back on itself.**

ɟ am

"I AM ADAPTABLE"

This is shown when the *I* **is curved and light in pressure and is of moderate size.**

Ɗ am

"I AM REFINED"

This is apparent when the *I* **is harmoniously formed and looks artistic.**

2 am

"I AM CAUTIOUS"

This is expressed by a **circle or an extended ending.**

"I AM DEMANDING"

This is seen in an *I that is large and takes up a lot of space.*

"I AM ACQUISITIVE"

This is expressed by an **inside hook and an inflated lower loop.**

"I AM ENERGETIC"

This is shown when the *I has any sweeping strokes, ascends upward, and is large in size.*

"I AM ENTHUSIASTIC"

This is expressed by an **ascending *I* underline made with heavy pressure.** It will be large in size and connected by a flourish to other words.

"I CAN CONFORM"

This can be identified when the ***I* is formed like the standard copybook *I*.**

"I AM SECOND-RATE"

This is expressed by the ***I* formed like the figure two.** This *I* is often produced by siblings who have not achieved as much as their brothers or sisters.

2 am

"I AM SELF-ABSORBED"

This is displayed by a **large upper loop** and reveals a man who will talk a lot about himself.

"I AM CONTRARY"

This is apparent when the shape of the *I* **is the reverse of the standard-form** *I***.**

"I AM COURAGEOUS"

This is expressed when the *I* **is tall and angular in form, large in size, and made with heavy pressure.**

"I AM FEARFUL"

This is shown when the *I* is **small and fragmented and shows uneven pressure.**

"I AM DEPRESSED"

This is indicated when the *I* is **small and tightly squeezed** and adheres closely to the baseline, or forms itself in a downward motion.

"I AM EMOTIONAL"

This is shown when the *I* is **small, acutely reclined, and heavy in pressure.**

"I AM IRRESPONSIBLE"

This is expressed when the *I* **goes back to the left.**

"I AM MODEST"

This is indicated by a **simple form of *I* or relatively small size.**

"I AM AN INTROVERT"

This is expressed when the ***I* is slanting more to the left** and gives an appearance of handwriting that is almost falling over.

"I AM AN EXTROVERT"

This is evidenced when the ***I* slants to the right.** The writer needs and likes people.

"I AM A LOOSE CANNON"

This is shown when the ***I* is on the far right and looks like it is about to fall over.** The writer always thinks of himself first.

"I AM RESERVED"

This is expressed by an *I* **that is vertical or that is squeezed or retraced and slants to the left.**

$\int$ am

"I AM MONEY HUNGRY"

This is displayed when the *I* **is shaped in the form of money or a number.**

$ am   8 am

"I AM A SHOW-OFF"

This is revealed by an **extremely large *I*, three to four times the height and width of the rest of the letters.** It is usually widely spaced and elaborately formed.

"I AM UNSOCIABLE"

This is expressed when the *I* **is unfinished or ill-formed.**

Iam   Iam

Six

Communication:

Express Yourself

HOW DOES THE writer communicate? Is he talkative or secretive? Is he open or evasive? Is he deceitful or honest? All these characteristics can be revealed before you invest valuable time and emotional commitment in the relationship. Many of the couples discussed later in this book (in "At the Stroke of Eleven"), married or united for eight years or more, express the importance of good communication and understanding. But what is good communication?

Communication between partners is more than just talking. It can take the form of body language, attitude, timing, respect, a look, a touch, a wink, or a simple gesture. Verbal communication can impart a sense of magic or romance by a note left under the pillow in your absence. Most important is respect and understanding and regard for the other person's feelings, opinions, and needs.

What seems effective with one person may not work in the same way with another, especially in times of conflict and stress. Are we being specific about our needs? How do we ask? Do we beg, demand, or expect our partners to know what is going on in our minds? Here are some of the characteristics that hinder communication and create problems within ourselves and in relationships. These are defense mechanisms to which we resort, hoping to get what we want when we don't quite know how to ask.

THE NONVERBAL COMMUNICATOR

Mr. Silent

He is indicated by the **closed *o*'s and *a*'s.** It will be hard to communicate with this man, because he tells you very little. Often he will give you only basic information—what you need to know and no more. The more you push him for information, the less likely he is to tell you. Tread gently. You need to know you cannot read his mind. Sometimes the silence of a partner can be as hurtful and painful as ranting and raving and use of a caustic tongue.

a O   *I said nothing to him*

Mr. Secretive

He identifies himself by the **loop on the right side of the circle on the top of the *o*'s and *a*'s.** He is a good confidant—you can tell him all your secrets—but watch out; he may not tell you all of his. He may find it hard to verbalize his own needs, especially if his handwriting slants to the left.

a O

Mr. Evasive

He identifies himself in handwriting by a **hook inside the
a's, *d*'s, and *o*'s.** This man may not always be direct with you.
He may hesitate when responding to a question. He will not
want to commit himself verbally until he can be sure that all
avenues are clear. He is not necessarily deceitful but he is
careful.

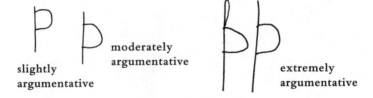

THE VOCAL COMMUNICATOR

Mr. Argumentative

He can be identified by the **stem extending at the top of
the *p*'s.** The higher the stem on the *p*, the more argumentative he will be. He will often spur on an intellectual debate.
No matter what you say, he will find a way to argue his point.
The only way you can win with an argumentative person is
to avoid him.

**slightly
argumentative**　　　**moderately
argumentative**　　　**extremely
argumentative**

Mr. Irritability

He reveals himself when the **dots of his *i*'s or *j*'s are re-
placed by jabs or by unusually short dashes** throughout
his writing. Irritability can be a combination of things: tired-

ness, discomfort, or sickness. Generally this man will be hard to get along with. Look for other characteristics such as argumentativeness and insecurity.

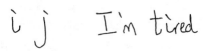

Mr. Aggressive/Assertive

He can be recognized when the **stems of the *g*'s, *j*'s, *p*'s, *q*'s, and *y*'s are farther from the upstroke.** The wider the space, the more aggressive he is. He is a go-getter. He will not wait for life to come to him. He will go out and find it, seek it, and enjoy it. He will step out and claim what is his. You may want to check his level of integrity to see how he will use these characteristics toward you.

Mr. Arrogant

This man's handwriting will express a combination of traits:

- unwarranted pride and self-importance, evidenced by very **tall *t* and *d* stems**
- self-interest, indicated by a **backward slant**
- a tendency to be domineering, revealed by **downward-pointing *t* bars**
- his strong ego is expressed by an extremely large **personal pronoun *I***

Mr. Direct-and-to-the-Point

His nature is expressed in **handwriting that is printed.** Printed handwriting usually means that the writer wants to be understood. He is factual and matter-of-fact about life in general. He usually distances himself from others. Sometimes printing can result from a professional habit, as in the case of architects and those who work on blueprints, or accountants.

Mr. Matter-of-Fact

This trait is expressed by the **final endings going downward in a rigid motion.** It can be seen in letters such as *d* and *e*. Like Mr. Direct, he won't spare your feelings, unless his handwriting is slanting to the right.

Mr. Bluff

He reveals himself in his handwriting by **heavy, blunt downstrokes** in letters such as *y, g, j, q,* and *p*. The thicker the downstroke, the more he is bluffing. So he told you that he could get your career off the ground because he has all these contacts. Don't wait for him to help you or to introduce you to anyone. You can probably pull more strings than he can. His ultimate goal may only be to pull your G-string.

Baby I got it

THE EFFECTIVE COMMUNICATOR

Mr. Listener

He reveals himself in handwriting by **open e's.** The listening type will be your counsel. He may never tell you how he feels, but will be happy to hear all that you have to say. For the talkative woman, this man is for you, especially if you are not really looking for answers.

Mr. Talkative

He shows himself in **open o's, a's, and d's.** This man will talk willingly and openly to you about anything and everything. His handwriting slants will determine how quickly he will respond to you. If his ego is a factor, he will brag and talk about himself, never concerning himself with you and your achievements.

a u I like to talk

Mr. Humorous

He is indicated by an **initial flourish at the beginning of a stroke.** This is a fun guy; no matter what, he will always see the humorous side to any obstacle or threatening situation. He will keep you smiling with his humor. In our troubled times, a man who can keep a smile on our faces is a man to keep around, don't you think?

my man is funny

Mr. Cautious

The **long, drawn-out ending of letters** expresses an extra level of caution. The longer the endings, the more cautious he will be. You will never get this man to rush into anything, especially if he is also ruled by his head and not his heart. Everything has to be thought through carefully and precisely before he makes a decision. If he is ruled by his emotions, he may be a little more spontaneous.

e a
Let's wait a while

Mr. Diplomat

This trait is indicated by the **second hump in his *m*'s being lower than the first hump.** He will be tactful in his responses to you, so watch carefully and try to read between the lines. He may be telling you *no* so politely it may not be clear to you that's what he really means.

Maybe we can meet
to mmorrow.

So how do you communicate?

How do you express yourself? Did you recognize yourself in the last few pages? What type of communicator appeals to you? Communication is an important factor in a relationship. Begin by saying what you mean and meaning what you say.

At the Stroke of . . .

Seven

Motivation: What Drives Him?

IS HE AMBITIOUS? A daydreamer? Someone who sets practical goals for himself? What drives him? How will he deal with all your burning ambitions? If he is not ambitious, can he handle your dreams and desires? His *t*'s will tell on him.

The higher his *t*'s are crossed, the higher the goals he sets for himself. The lower his *t*'s are crossed, the lower the goals. If he's not particularly ambitious and you have high-level career demands, you need someone who is confident within himself and is not threatened by your goals. (See "At the Stroke of Five.")

Mr. Ambitious

T bars are crossed and placed high on the stem in this man's case. He has set high but practical goals for himself. (Contributing characteristics reinforcing his goals could be acquisitiveness, good self-esteem, and determination.) Remember that every characteristic can have another that will strengthen or weaken its value. Your man may cross his *t*'s high and be enthusiastic, but if in his sample there is evidence of procrastination and laziness, these traits will diminish his level of ambition.

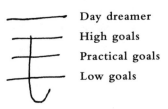

Day dreamer
High goals
Practical goals
Low goals

Mr. Strong-Willed

He can be recognized when the *t* **bars are thicker than the stem.** The thicker the bar, the stronger the will. This man has a purpose in life. With his strong will and enthusiasm, he can achieve a great deal.

Mr. Enthusiastic

He reveals himself by long *t* **bars sweeping through several letters,** indicative of the drive and force that keep him going. It helps the man persuade others to do what he wants. You may not agree with his plan, but his emotion can often sweep you off your feet.

Mr. Optimist

He can be detected when the *t* **bar goes upward or when the handwriting goes upward.** While enthusiasm is a driving force, optimism is realistic and makes him stick to the task even in the face of adversity.

Mr. Disciplined

A *t* **bar bowed downward,** like an arrow, is a sign of this man.

If he has strong feelings for you, he may have a hard time showing it. He keeps his feelings tightly locked away so you are unable to detect what is going on inside him. However, if his writing slants to the right, his emotions will temper some of his self-control.

Mr. Determined

A **straight downstroke in the *g*'s and *y*'s,** looped or not, indicates stamina, determination, and energy. The longer the downward tail, the stronger the drive and stamina. Determination is the stamina and drive behind willpower.

Mr. Persistent

Knots in *f*'s, *p*'s, *h*'s, and *t*'s show persistence.

If at first the writer doesn't succeed, he will try, try again. If you don't want him around, you may have difficulty getting him to understand that. He will find different ways to attract your attention.

$$f \quad f \quad h \quad P$$

Mr. Acquisitive

This man is a go-getter. An **initial hook at the beginning of letters** indicates the desire and will to acquire what he wants. He is not necessarily a materialist but has a strong desire to achieve a goal. This trait involves drive, motivation, and determination.

$$A \quad a \qquad We \ can \ acquire \ anything$$

Mr. Tenacious

This man goes the extra mile and holds on tightly to his beliefs. A **hook at the ending of letters** indicates the desire to hold on to what he has.

$$T \quad t \qquad hold \ on \ tightly$$

Mr. *Organized*

A balanced *f,* **which has loops on the top and bottom of equal size,** is the first sign of an organized man.

A balanced *f*

The spaces between lines are your second signal. The organized man will probably want all his clothes and yours in order, probably color-coded too. He will plan his week and his time with you carefully. If his handwriting is slanted to the right, he will be a little more spontaneous.

Mr. *Responsible*

He expresses himself in handwriting by **large circles at the beginning of letters.** This man will want to get involved with everything and everybody. Look for contributing traits such as determination, practical goals, organizational ability, pride, and purpose.

Mr. *Positive*

This trait is evidenced when the **downstroke of the stem of a letter is straight.** Look at *t*'s, *l*'s, and *h*'s. Mr. Positive is a little like Mr. Optimist. He takes advantage of positive thought to get him through.

LACK OF MOTIVATION?

We now move on to discover traits representing a lack of ambition and motivation.

You may often see *t* **bars of different heights and varying forms** in the same handwriting sample. Always make your decision based on the majority.

For instance, you have forty *t* bars in a sample of handwriting:

18 *t* bars crossed high = ambition
7 *t* bars crossed full length across the word = enthusiasm
15 *t* bars crossed on the left-hand side = procrastination

The first two types of *t* bars show a high level of motivation from which must be subtracted the fifteen signs of procrastination. Do you still think this person is ambitious with the amount of procrastination evident in his script?

Then look at other characteristics that would support his determination, enthusiasm, and willpower, and finally, look at characteristics that reduce the level of his motivation.

Mr. No Aspirations

When his *t* **bars are crossed low on the stem,** the writer sets low goals for himself and is not a high achiever. (He may

even underestimate his abilities.) Look at his personal pronoun *I* to see how he views himself. This could be an indica-
tor of whether his goals are practical or if there are other
warning signs of trouble ahead.

Mr. Daydreamer

When the *t* **bar does not connect to the stem,** the writer
is sometimes not in touch with reality. He is an armchair
planner. This man may have a million ideas in his head but is
unable to follow through on them. Additional traits such as
procrastination will also reduce his drive for achieving his
dreams. If he promises you a house with a pool, be sure you
look for characteristics that can help him to achieve it. Or go
get a house with a pool yourself, and don't wait for him.

Mr. Weak Will

If the *t* **bar is thinner than the stem,** the will of the writer
is weak. He has no backbone. His willpower will buckle as
soon as he is faced with any major obstacles.

Mr. Fickle/Irresponsible

The *t* **bar bowed in the middle of the stem** is a sign of this man. He may make you promises but will prove unable to deliver on them, not intentionally, but just because he is a little bit fickle. At the time he made his promise he may have been sincere, but his ideals and ideas may change from day to day. He may turn up late or forget he had to meet you. His approach to life is usually one of very little commitment. He thinks the grass is always greener on the other side. So watch out. He may be dating another lady on the other side of town.

Mr. Stubborn

The **stem of this man's *t* is double.** The smaller the handwriting or the **wider the stem separation at the bottom of the *t*,** the more stubborn he will be. Other indicators of stubborn are *t*'s **that are shaped like the star of David or have a triangle on the left side of the stem.** Stubborn also can be seen in the **wide-open stems of *d*'s.** If this man says no, he means no. The more you try to get him to do something, the more he will dig his heels in the ground and act like a stubborn mule.

Mr. Procrastinator

T **bars crossed on the left side of the stem** are the sign of a procrastinator, as are *i* **dots crossed on the left side of the *i* stem.**

He likes the word *mañana* (tomorrow). He promised you that he would marry you last year, and near the end of this year there is still no sign of a ring. Sometimes you just have to give this man a jump start. Either that, or move on if you cannot wait for him to fulfill his promises.

lets start tomorrow

Mr. Disorganized

This trait is shown in the **unbalanced *f*—either the upper or lower loop is uneven.** If the lines are overlapping and there is very little spacing between the lines, confusion is added. Have some mercy.

Mr. No Determination

Short stems in the *g*'s and *y*'s whether there is a loop or not indicate this man. When the going gets tough, Mr. No Determination will jump ship quickly.

Mr. Greedy

This trait is expressed by the **large hook on the beginning of any letters, especially capitals.** If you see deceit or other characteristics that reduce his level of integrity, keep your personal finances private and personal. He may assume what is yours is automatically his too.

Lady Luck

Mr. Leisure

This man betrays his character by **double-stem *b*'s, *t*'s, and *d*'s, and slow and deliberate handwriting.** He will do everything in his own time. Do not try to rush him. He has two speeds: slow and stop.

I am busy doing nothing

Mr. Fatalism

This trait is expressed by the **ending stroke curling down-ward at the end of letters such as *d, e, g, w,* and *y*.**

yp d e g

At the Stroke of . . .

Eight

Mental Process:

What Is He Thinking?

EVERY WOMAN WANTS a man with a good head on his shoulders, doesn't she? One of the most stimulating parts of a man's body and his most important feature is his . . . no, try looking up. We will get to that other part later (in "At the Stroke of Nine"). Look at his uppermost part—behind his eyes.

We may spend so much time concentrating on a man's looks, his biceps, his butt, that we may forget that he can actually think. However, an intelligent man can be a bore if he has not learned how to be humble and laugh at himself sometimes. It is a matter of knowing, but not letting everyone know how much you know. It's a question of humility.

One of my husband's greatest assets is his stimulating conversation. He has kept me on my toes over the years. If I don't know something, I can depend on him for the answer. He can explain it without being arrogant or patronizing.

As he is a man of few words, I am always in awe when I hear him explain something quite clearly to our son or one of his peers. He varies his vocabulary, depending on the person he is talking to. He missed his vocation; he should have been a teacher. However, making decisions can be a little more of a challenge for him, as he needs all the facts and wants all questions answered before he decides on a path of action.

We are all works in progress. At any given time in our lives something could change us, make us angry, intolerant, depressed, or less understanding. A death, a missing child, or an illness—all these can change our attitude toward life.

How often have we tried to read someone's mind? It can be done through handwriting analysis. How information is received and processed is important in communicating and building a stronger personal relationship. You can often be at odds because of a simple misunderstanding.

Here are four ways a man may process information. Which one are you dealing with?

Mr. Analytical

He can be recognized by **_v_ formations in middle-zone letters such as _m_'s, _n_'s, and the lower part of _h_'s.** No matter which way you turn this sample, these letters will look like _v_'s. The wider and taller the _v_ formations, the more analytical the writer will be.

This man is the "Why?" person. He does not accept anything at face value. He will question everything. He is not easily fooled. His questioning may irritate you, especially if you are a superficial thinker and quite content with surface knowledge. It is hard to play games with this man.

My "Why?" MINᗡ

Mr. Methodical

This man can be recognized by the **rounded *m*'s and *n*'s and the lower part of *h*'s.** The formation of letters is a slow process with him. He needs to build on all the facts. He wants information in a logical sequence. He understands best from demonstration rather than explanation and may appear slow to you at times. The lack of speed in which he receives information has nothing to do with his IQ. His method of processing information may be irritating to you if you are quick at grasping information. Be patient with this man. He needs time to accumulate all his information before he responds to you. It may even seem to you that he is not paying attention when you are together. Yet he is listening to every word you are saying. He just needs plenty of time before he responds. Allow him that.

My mind builds all the facts

Mr. Superficial

This man can be identified by **ill-formed letters almost threadlike** in appearance. He tends to rely on superficial knowledge. He skims the surface, extracting what is important to him. This may be useful in extracting the essence of something, but danger may lie in failure to understand the deeper ramifications of what he has processed in his mind.

Surface Knowledge in for me

Mr. Quick and Sharp

This man can be recognized by the **pointed tops of his *m*'s, *n*'s, and *h*'s.** He is a fast thinker. He grasps knowledge quickly and assesses information without much explanation.

Mr. Initiative

This trait is expressed with **v-shaped *h*'s.** You can rely on this man to make the first move. If his handwriting slants to the right, he will be spontaneous in his actions.

So, which type are you? How do you process information? Now that we have discovered the four aspects of processing information, how does your prospective partner make a decision?

DECISIONS: WILL HE MARRY ME, OR WON'T HE?

When it comes to making a decision, how long will he take?

Mr. Decisive

This is indicated when the *t* **bar has a thick ending.**

The decisive man will need no help from you to make up his mind. You may be the one who is undecided. If the man is ruled by his emotions, he may make snap decisions without you.

t   let's do it

Mr. Indecisive

This man's *t* **bar starts out thick but fades out at the end.** You may need to give him some help, especially if he is a methodical thinker and ruled by logic.

I don't know yet

Mr. Hesitant

You can recognize him by **dots at the beginning of a stroke, or a lead stroke on letters such as** *h***.** He places his pen on the paper; his mind pauses, and so does his pen, leaving a spot at the beginning of the initial stroke. He will need time. If he is ruled by his emotions, his handwriting will slant to the right. The hesitation indicated here can actually be the reins to slow down his impulsive tendencies.

Wait a minute

Mr. Fickle

Saucer-shaped *t* bars are a sign of this man. Watch out for him. He will send you mixed messages all the time. Fickle men are usually unreliable and shallow, though with no evil intentions. They may agree on something one day with every intention of doing it. However, call him back in a few weeks, and you will discover that his plans have changed and he has already rescheduled your time with him. Theater tickets are not a good start with this man.

Mr. Worrier

Worry can be revealed by **loops in the *m*, the *n*, and the *w*.** Worrying is an extension of the imagination. What does worry do? Nothing but sap precious energy.

My money will not meet
her needs

CREATIVE AND IMAGINATIVE TYPES

Mr. Imaginative

The **bigger his loops,** the more imagination this man has. The smaller the loops, the more restricted his imagination is.

Imagination is shown by the loops in both the upper and lower zones. Length reveals the degree of energy and determination, and width shows the degree of imagination. Imagination can be an advantage or a liability. For example, imagination combined with deceit may produce a compulsive liar. Imagination combined with creativity and determination can produce a fanciful character who blows things out of proportion. Excessive imagination may lead to exaggeration.

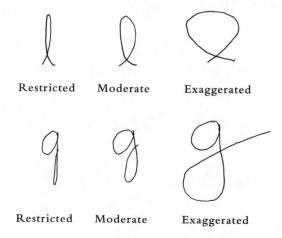

| Restricted | Moderate | Exaggerated |

| Restricted | Moderate | Exaggerated |

This is evidence of how he organizes his work:

creates ideas

follows
through on
his ideas

Mr. Creative

His handwriting is characterized by **flat-topped r's.** This man can think on his feet and has good mental and physical coordination. He is often musical or ambidextrous. If he is good with his hands, then get him to apply them to your body for wonderful massages.

Mr. Vocalist

This trait is shown by the **loop on the right side of the r's.** You can rely on this man to burst into song.

Two loops evident at the top of the r's indicate this man will be willing to sing to you and others.

As shown by the **small loop on the left of the r,** this man may be a little reluctant to create a scene but you may often find him singing to himself.

Mr. Book Lover

The book lover is revealed by his **e's looking like a backward 3 and his delta-shaped d's.** If you enjoy joining all the latest book clubs and attending poetry readings, you will want to find a partner with this kind of handwriting: An added plus in any man's personality.

Mr. Spiritual

The height of letters such as *l, b, d, k, t,* and *h* extending upward indicates this man. The higher they are, the more this man is reaching for a higher philosophical and spiritual understanding. However, you must look for clear, clean formations in the *o*'s and *a*'s, which express communication, and check that all characteristics representing integrity are present.

Spiritual light

Mr. Smooth

Fluidity can be revealed in handwriting by **easily formed letters that look like the figure 8, especially in the *g*'s and *y*'s,** and also by a ***t* stroke running into the connecting letters, such as *h*.** A man with this kind of writing is flexible. He can communicate with ease and process information readily. He is quick with his words and his hands and can talk himself out of any sticky situation.

I send to my Darling
Daughter love & kisses wishing success of every thing that's good. I will now say bye-bye until I hear from you.

Your Loving

OTHER TYPES

Mr. Entrepreneur

This man is revealed by the **open *b*,** which is known as the
business *b.* An entrepreneur in the making; look at his *t*'s to
tell whether he can carry out his goals or if he is a dreamer.

Mr. Meticulous

You often hear it said: Be careful to cross your *t*'s and dot your
i's. The **closer the meticulous man's *i* dots are to the
stem,** the more attention to detail he has. The farther the *i*
dot is from the stem, the less attention to detail he has. Don't
think you can go on a date with this man with a run in your
panty hose. You won't get away with it. He will notice that
and more, right down to the color of your toenail polish.
Make sure it's not chipped.

Mr. Perfection

Clues to his character are similar to Mr. Meticulous's: **even
margins, balanced *t* bars** throughout the handwriting,
even spacing, and **low *t* bars** positioned to show his goals.
This man will insist on doing everything to the highest degree of excellence. He is usually self-disciplined and needs

approval for a perfect job. He can be highly competitive. He is a high achiever, inclined to meet deadlines. If you are the flighty type, this man will surely drive you crazy.

Since I've been back I've hardly cut double the amount of work next week Saturday we're havin thats going to stop me from rly time when I get to have exciting has happened yet. In a be seeing the 'A' version of

Mr. Forgetful

This man's handwriting is indicated by **i's without dots or far away from the i stem.** Mr. Forgetful overlooks trivia or details he feels to be unimportant. While birthdays and special dates may be important to you, he will not value these dates or take the time to try to make a mental note of them and other occasions that matter to you. If he is a superficial thinker, he will have only basic information.

I didn't remember

Mr. Self-Critical

This man reveals himself by a **small c placed over the i stem rather than a dot.** He is quick to pass judgment on himself and, as in the case of the perfectionist, nothing is ever

good enough for him. To discover to what degree he is critical, look for associated traits such as sarcasm, resentment, and
a domineering attitude. Perhaps, however, he may have an
ability to soften his critical nature in a diplomatic and constructive way.

KEEP IN MIND

The possibility of a learning disability can often be determined by **ill-formed letters.** Please handle this man with
care.

Energy and Sex Drive

IN MY ENDEAVOR to be fair to men, I carried out a survey, interviewing more than five hundred men from various backgrounds about their needs and what they want from women. They were unanimous in the view that men want as much sex as they can get. Now let us see how much energy and sex drive they actually have.

Earlier, in "At the Stroke of Two," we looked at zones and identified the lower zone as being the area of energy, stamina, and drive. The bottom line is, if you want someone with high energy and endless sex drive, you must look in his lower zones. I told you we'd get to it.

The longer the tails in the *g*'s and *y*'s, the longer the writer's stamina, drive, and energy ("I'll take you all the way, baby! I'll rock your world!"). It's that simple!

If the physical side of a relationship is paramount to you, and you want lots of passion, you should look for **long g's and y's** in a man's handwriting. Look also at your own level of energy and stamina to see if you and your partner are a good match. Are you compatible with his drive or lack of it? If he says he can take you all the way, he had better have **long g and y tails** in his script. Mr. Quickie will have the shorter g and y tails. The shorter they are, the less energy he has to perform.

Oh no! not again tonight

Mr. Lover Man

He is indicated by a **complete g in full balance,** with no exaggerated loops or oversized middle zones. He is the perfect lover, a warm person who is able to find contentment with one partner.

g   good guys

Mr. Sensuous

There are several traits that represent this type of man. He uses **thick, pasty strokes,** as if the handwriting were written with a felt-tipped pen. The writing may be **blotchy, with parts of the letters covered** (especially the e's and the a's) as if done with a bad ink pen.

The sensuous man will be very tactile and extravagant. His desires will be strong and he will want to indulge you in all the wonders of his world. His senses will drive you wild. He loves good food and wine; he is totally self-indulgent. Whether he can afford this or not will be hard to tell in the initial stages. If you don't see him often, that could be your clue. He may be saving up for the next sensual extravaganza.

Sensuous

I'm keeping their picture and one other of you. Please pardon the pad but I don't write very many letters these days. I do however intend to maintain contact with you and I'll get a writing pad. Again the contact is my pleasure and I look forward to seeing you.

Mr. Conceited

This man is vain and has an exaggerated opinion of himself that he will expect you to share. This trait is revealed in **exceedingly tall *t* and *d* stems.**

I am not a bedroom bore

Mr. Sexual Peacock

This man's **capital letters will extend in long tails either below the next name or the next part of the same name.** Long before you see his handwriting you will recognize him visually. The sexual peacock struts around with his chest out, confident and self-assured. Beware. He may not necessarily be a good lover. Remember to check the length of his *y*'s and *g*'s.

MR   Lover Man

Mr. Self-Centered

This man's handwriting reveals a high level of vanity and egotism. His **capitals will be three times larger** than the rest of his words. He will write his name larger than the other words and the personal pronoun *I* will be longer. The self-centered lover is very much caught up in himself. He is the principal object of his affection and doesn't really need you to be there or to love him. Your feelings and needs may go totally unmet, owing to his insensitivity. If you left him and didn't return, he would not understand what he had done to make you go. He would probably believe that you were the one at fault or did not appreciate him. He would consider it your loss, not his.

I am so Great

Mr. Nervous

He reveals himself in handwriting by **disconnections in letters, particularly *r*'s and *k*'s.** You need to look at his ego and his level of esteem and how he feels about himself.

You will need to take time and be gentle with him. Don't criticize him and don't be too assertive, or you may chase him away.

Kate lets bizeak the Rules

Mr. Talkative

This man writes **wide-open *o*'s, *a*'s, and *d*'s.** He will want to keep you constantly informed about how he is feeling and what he will be doing next. Nothing will surprise you. He takes communication to another level. Before you are undressed you will already know what to expect. He's the type that will want you to call out his name. As if he doesn't know it! Ladies, you know the type.

d d d o g y

Mr. Frustrated

This man's nature is expressed in handwriting by a ***g* or *y* with an ascending line that nearly always fails to reach the middle zone.** There may be many reasons for this. If the handwriting is slanting to the left, the man is reserved; it may be hard for him to approach you. If his handwriting slants to the right, he may be too impulsive, saying all the wrong things and driving you away. You should investigate other characteristics, such as self-confidence, communication, and emotions.

Mr. Night Nurse

This trait is indicated by the **hourglass formation on the lower loop.** He may have a tendency to be clinical and uncaring. The Night Nurse gives the injection and leaves, rarely staying the entire night.

Mr. Selfish

This trait is expressed with a **straight downstroke.** He will initiate sex only when he wants it. He won't accommodate your needs, because he doesn't know how and doesn't care.

Mr. Irresponsible

This trait is shown in the **bottom of the *g*'s and *y*'s in an arc shape.** He may not want to wear a condom. Protection will be your responsibility, not his.

SOME QUIRKS

Mr. Angry and Sexually Aggressive

These traits are shown in the **angular hook at the bottom of the tail.**

Mr. Denial of Sexual Pleasure

This trait is evidenced by the **retracing of the downward stroke.** The writer may repress his sexual urges.

Mr. Seeking Security

The **downstroke is retraced and moves to the right,** indicating that the writer is the dependent type and seeks security. He may want someone to lean on.

Mr. Unsettled Libido

This is revealed by **too much variety in the form, length, or direction of writing.**

Mr. Unusual Sexual Desire

This is expressed when the **downstrokes end in a squiggle.**

Mr. Exaggerated Overemphasis on Sex

This trait is shown by a **wide, exaggerated lower loop.** The bigger the loop, the more exaggerated the act.

Mr. Cock of the Walk

The **angled and looped downstrokes** express his sexual vanity. He is the type that wants all the lights on so you can see his glory.

Mr. Four Times a Day

This is indicated by **heavy pressure with inflated lower loops.**

Mr. Suppressed Sexual Urges

He is revealed by **reversed endings,** showing that he suppresses his urges by doing other things than taking part in the sex act.

Mr. Only the Chase

His **upstrokes stop short,** which shows that he enjoys only the chase—the kill may be too much for him.

Mr. Nonverbal Mover

Very narrow loops reveal his inability to express his needs.

Mr. Sexual Agility

When his **downstrokes start with light pressure and his upstrokes end with heavy pressure,** he may take a long time to get started. However, this partner could be full of surprises with his sexual agility.

Mr. Stroker

When the **tail of the *g* or the *y* is straight with a leftward stroke,** don't count on him to please you. Self-gratification is enough for him.

Mr. Bossy

In this man's case, look for *t* bars that are pointed downward and stroke endings that are thick and blunt. He may be physically abusive and try to dominate you both verbally and physically. No matter what you do, it may not please him. Avoid him. This is a no-win situation.

Mr. Sexual Aggressor

Sexual deviance or dominance is indicated in handwriting that shows **sharp-angled triangles in the *g*'s and *y*'s.** A study carried out on rapists in prison showed that a high percentage of inmates made the letters *y* and *g* in a triangular form. This represents a high level of concentration on the female area of the body, and therefore aggression toward women. With a combination of dominance and sensuousness, your date could go terribly wrong. The man may pounce on you before you are ready to be intimate with him, not accepting no for an answer.

SAMPLES FROM CONVICTED SEX OFFENDERS

- Dominance is evident in the *t* **bars crossed downward.**
- Deceit is shown in the **loops inside the *o*'s and *a*'s.**
- Tension is shown in the **letters squeezed together** (note the *y* and *e* in *lawyers*, the *e* and *r* in *therapy*, and the *g* and *o* in *going*).

· Unpredictability is indicated in the **uneven letter size.**
Look at the first *y* in the first sentence and the last *y* in the
last word.

*Sexual assault
on a adult.*

*went to the lawyers office, an they sent us
to the doctor's office. We've been going to thupy
every since. Other than that everything is
going okay.*

Arrested for Fondling His Daughter

· Supersensitivity is expressed by the **large loops in the *d*'s.**
· The controlled baseline is evidence of inflexibility.
· Domination is shown by *t* **bars written downward.**
· Deceit is expressed by the **loops inside the *o*'s and *a*'s.**
· Underestimation of self is shown by the *t* **bars crossed
low.**
· Temperamentalness is expressed by the **uneven letter size.**
· Repression is shown by the **retraced letters,** such as *h*'s
and *b*'s.

*Here it is another week has gome by I th
God each and every day that goes by. I have
be very thankful for all he has done for me. I
a blessing just to be out here and most lichi*

Physically Abused His Stepchild

- Deceit is shown by the **double loops inside o's and a's.**
- Oversensitivity is expressed by the **large loops in the d's and t's.**
- Domination is shown by the **t bars crossed downward.**
- Compulsive lying is indicated by the **figure eight inside the o.**

Today when I was out side I received a phone call from my Dad and I was really suprised when he told me that he and my mother who was hurt before

Attempted Aggravated Rape with Use of a Gun

- Deceit is expressed by the **loops in the o's and a's.**
- Domination is evident by the **t bars crossed downward.**
- Controlling and inflexible traits are expressed by an **even baseline.**
- Sensitivity to criticism is shown by the **loops in the t's and d's.**

I had a very enjoiable day at the shelter. Fred and I went and pick up some shirts for me to wear. The work was fine and it was good having the people back from vacation

Arrested for Stalking His Wife with Phone Calls and
Threats of Suicide

· Jealousy is indicated by **circles at the beginning of let-
  ters, in this case the *m*'s.**
· Domination is shown in the *t* **bars crossing downward.**
· Intensity is indicated by the **small script.**

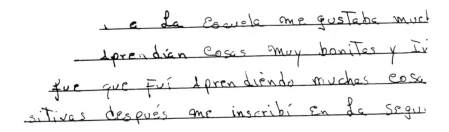

WHAT MEN WANT

Since this book is about finding the right man, I interviewed
more than five hundred men to find out what they really
wanted. My survey consisted of men of varying nationalities,
professions, and ages. The outstanding lesson I learned is that
they are just as vulnerable as women. Ninety percent of them
admitted to having their heart broken sometime after the age
of twenty-one. Some admitted they are still on the road to re-
covery. They tread just as carefully and cautiously as we do.
One man said his heart was broken every day. Another said
every time a relationship does not work out, his heart is broken. Their experiences have made them skeptical and cautious of women. However, they tend to handle their
disappointments and hurt differently, by having several relationships at once. There is safety in numbers.

A large proportion of the men want sex, sex, and more sex, as often as they can get it. Throw in some food and some sports activity, and they are happy. Caribbean men seemed to be more conservative in their approach to sex than men of other backgrounds. African-American men and white males were more adventurous and given to experimentation.

Answers to some of the questions are as follows:

1. What attracts you most in a woman?
   a) Sex appeal
   b) Intelligence
   c) Money status
   d) Spirituality
   e) Other
   80% said sex appeal, 10% intelligence, 5% money status, 3% spirituality, 2% other.

2. Is the chase better than the kill?
   85% loved the chase and found it exhilarating and exciting. 15% hated the chase and found it frustrating. They didn't like the games women play.

3. Have you ever chased a woman and been disappointed with the kill?
   70% have been disappointed with the final kill.

4. If she is aggressive, do you like it?
   40% liked a sexually aggressive woman; 50% preferred her to be in control and lead the way; 10% didn't mind it once or twice but preferred to be in control themselves.

5. How long do you expect to wait before being intimate when you start dating?

75% wanted sex as soon as possible but were not pushy on early dates; the average time given was two months.

6. If you get sex on the first date, do you respect her less?
95% would *not* respect her less.

7. What turns you on most about a woman?
The answers varied. Here are the top four:
a) "My pregnant partner."
b) "A woman with presence."
c) "Nipples subtly revealed"
d) Groomed pubic hairs.

8. What turns you off?
80% said lack of intelligence, followed by vulgarity, those who talk BS, those who have no style, and teasers.

9. How many women have you dated at one time?
80% had dated up to three women at one time.

10. When is fidelity important?
The general consensus was that fidelity is important when there is a mutual agreement about commitment from both parties. (One man asked me on whose side, not considering that I may have meant him.)

11. Have you had group sex?
80% had been involved with 2 or more other people at once.

12. What is the worst thing you have done to a woman?
These are some of the confessions:
a) Gave a woman a sexually transmitted disease.
b) Had sex with two women within hours. While one

was leaving through the back door, the other was coming in the front.

c) Ran out of money while on a date and went to another woman's house to get money, then had oral sex with the other woman before returning to his date.

13. Have you ever slept with your woman's best friend, girlfriend, or sister?

    85% admitted to this act. One man even explained the reason for this: the best friend, girlfriend, or sister, he said, was the closest person to his woman, and he felt he had to break that bond so as to have something over the other woman. One man confessed that he was forced into it.

14. How often do you want sex? Three times a night, every night, or three times a week?

    80% said every night.

15. How long do you want to date before you get married?

    80% said approximately two years to be safe.

16. What is your ultimate sexual fantasy?

    The most popular fantasy was having two women, or watching two or more women, followed by making love in a plane, which was followed by making love at the peak of Kilimanjaro (or another well-known height).

17. Have you ever had your heart broken? If yes, has it made you bitter, cautious, or skeptical?

    95% said proudly that they had, but it made them cautious, not skeptical or bitter. Their intent is not to hurt

women. One man said infidelity was an armor for his
protection.

18. Did your relationship with your mother hinder or en-
    hance your relationship with women?
    75% said it enhanced their relationships with women;
    20% said it hindered; 5% said they were raised by men.

19. Have you ever had sex with a prostitute?
    80% said yes.

20. Have you ever been paid for sex?
    60% said yes.

21. What part of a woman's body do you like the most?
    75% said legs; 15% said breasts; 10% said the whole body.

22. What do you like the most sexually?
    Oral sex scored highest, at 80%.

23. What is the maximum time you can survive without sex?
    Responses varied from two weeks to one year. 70% said
    one month is the maximum, but tried to avoid any
    time out.

24. If you were a woman, what type of man would you
    want?
    Most men described men different from themselves.

25. What is the most valuable lesson you have learned from
    a woman?
    The importance of becoming a father (which they just
    can't do without a woman), followed by being more
    careful and cautious with their feelings.

26. What would you tell your daughter about men?

Most often said: "Use your head." Next were "Be intuitive" and "Listen to your head and not your heart."

27. Which foods do you like to play with during sex?
80% were willing to try anything their partner liked. Favorites were honey, whipped cream, and fruit.

28. What is your favorite time of day?
75% said happy hour, after work; 25% said after 9 P.M.

29. What is your favorite holiday?
The holiday varied, depending on religion and culture. 60% said Christmas; 20% said Thanksgiving; 20% mentioned other holidays such as Halloween and Kwanza.

30. What gifts would you like to receive?
80% said flowers and gifts that are handmade, or gifts to which a great deal of thought was given in the preparation or choosing; 20% said clothes.

31. What gifts do you hate to receive?
Most often cited were tacky gifts to which no thought was given, e.g., colognes, socks, ties.

32. Which places do you hate to be taken to?
Most often cited were malls, movies, and places where they are surrounded by unintelligent people.

33. What's the best BS line that works for you?
Most men said they didn't have a BS line. They said what came naturally to them in any given situation.

34. Must she be able to cook?
90% want a woman to be able to cook because they can too. They don't expect a woman to cook for them all

the time, but they prefer her to know how to do it. One man said, "As long as she can read, she should be able to cook."

35. Do you prefer a natural woman or a made-up woman?
     80% preferred a natural woman. One man referred to the made-up woman as "weave, wig-wearing wonders—www.com."

36. Which is most important, your own orgasm or hers?
     60% said hers; 25% said their own; 15% said it didn't matter as long as both parties were having fun.

37. Are sex toys essential or a waste of time?
     Many liked variation and thought toys added new spice to the relationship but didn't think they were essential.

At the Stroke of . . .

Ten

The Secrets in His Signature

A MAN'S SIGNATURE is his personal thumbprint and can tell a lot about him. Whereas his personal pronoun *I* reveals his private self-image, his signature uncovers his public image, the way he wants his public to know him. Although a signature can tell you something about your man, you should not rely on it totally, without an additional sample to help you form a complete picture of him. There should be some similarities between the sample writing and the signature. A difference in the two may indicate some discord in his personality.

Many people practice with various signatures, particularly in their teenage years, searching for one that will best represent them and that is easy to write. The signature often will change as their circumstances and needs change. How the writer feels about his family, particularly his parents, is often evident in his signature.

I often hear my clients say, "My signature changes all the time." Yes, it is supposed to change. One of the easiest ways to determine forgery is when a signature looks exactly the same, as if it had been copied.

Mr. Self-Reliant

An **underscore under the name** represents a man who is independent and self-reliant. More than one underscore indicates that self-reliance is extremely strong. In his hour of need he may never call on you for help or advice. He has carried out his activities alone for so long that now that he has someone else in his life, it is hard for him to say, "I need you."

Mr. Flamboyant

This man reveals his nature by **large, flamboyant letters** in his name and **embellished letters** elsewhere. I am always concerned when I see too many flourishes in writing. They mean that the writer wants to be noticed and recognized. If he chooses to spend so much time concerned about his name, you can imagine how little time he will have to notice you. He is too obsessed with his own self-importance.

Mr. Modest

He is revealed by a **small signature,** which, however, should be in balance with the size of his script. He doesn't want to stand out in a crowd and prefers to stay backstage while others take his praise and kudos.

Mr. "I Must Have the Last Word"

A **period at the end** of the signature indicates a man who must have the last word. Check to see if argumentativeness is evident in the script. This factor strengthens the characteristic.

Mr. Nurturing

When the **signature is encircled,** it shows that the person is protective, especially toward those to whom he is close. You will be safe and secure with this man. Look for other qualities such as loyalty and security.

Mr. Genuine

You can recognize this man when you can **read both names clearly and they are written in full.** He has no hidden agenda. What you see is what you get. He is open and available to nearly everyone. If you are the passive type, you will have a hard time dealing with his constant availability to others.

Morgan Smith

Mr. Family Man

His character is revealed when the **last name is bigger than the first name.** He is bonded to his family or has been an integral part of it, thus far. He puts his family before himself. Sometimes, if the family name has status or clout, this could also be a factor in its size.

John Smith

Mr. Me First

He can be recognized when the **first name is larger than the last name.** He considers himself before his family. This could also express a discord in his relationship with his father or lack of a paternal influence.

Mike wright

Larger script only in the name indicates the writer looks for recognition and could be hiding his true feelings of inferiority.

Yours Sincerely

John Smith.

Mr. Self-Protective

He makes a **line above and below his name.** He is looking out for himself and does not trust others.

Chuck Ellis

Mr. Protective

If he has a *t* in his name, the *t* **bar extends over the rest of the letters.** He is protective toward his family and friends.

Barrett Wilson

Mr. No Confidence

He makes a **line through his name.** He has a low self-image, or there may be some discord with his father or the name he carries, representing his family.

Mr. Optimist

There is an **upward slant** to his signature. He always has a cheerful approach to life.

Rick Taylor

Mr. Depressed

He reveals his nature by a **downward-slanting signature.** He may be depressed or just tired at the time of writing. If the rest of the text is written downward also, there is strong evidence of depression. Don't forget to check the pressure of the script; if too thick or too heavy, he is in deep pain.

Wilson Smith

Mr. Cautious

This man writes only the **initial letter of his first name,** followed by his last name. He is cautious until he is sure of himself and sure of you.

M. Nelson

Mr. Humor

A sense of humor is shown by a **wavy initial stroke on letters such as *m*'s and *n*'s or wavy underlining in general.**

Martin Nelson

Mr. Familiar

An **elaborate underline** beneath a man's name shows famil-
iarity. The writer may want to be on a first-name basis or use
a nickname with you before you are ready for that.

QUIZ

Now that you have all the facts and samples before you, here
is a little exercise for you to practice on. Each of these two
men sent you an invitation for a date. One looks like Denzel
Washington and the other like Matthew McConaughey, and
you can choose to go anywhere, anytime on your date, with
all expenses paid. Which man would you feel safer spending
your evening with, A or B?

A — *I'm really not much of a sport's fan, but I think that the ▇▇▇▇▇ 's did poorly, because of poor coaching! I'm very much against the areana deal because, it will (coas) cost the public and not the team*

B — *No offense intended with the way I opened this letter. I could think of no other proper way to start a letter to a lady whose name I've yet to have the pleasure of knowing.*

Your answer should be: B.

B: Mr. Good Guy

Although the handwriting of Mr B. is messy, this is the good guy. You can count on him.

· His spontaneous side is expressed by his **right slant.**
· High energy is shown by the **long lower-zone letters g and y.**
· His **thick t bars** are evidence of his strong will.
· Determination is shown in the **long g's and y's.**
· Although his handwriting is messy, the **baseline** suggests he is optimistic and flexible.
· The **upper loops** extending upward show his level of ethics and morals.
· He is a proud individual, shown by the **long-stem d's.**
· The **balance of upper and lower zones** expresses a balanced personality.

A: Mr. Not-So-Good Guy

Now let us look closely at the warning signs in sample A. Here are some red flags:

· **Large loops in the lower zone, shown in his f's and g's,** suggest high energy and sex drive.
· A desire to be noticed is evident in the **loops at the top of the t's and final strokes that turn upward.**
· Fickle/irresponsible traits are shown by *t* **bars dipped** in the center of the stem.
· Inflexibility is expressed by the **controlled and straight baseline.**

- An idealist is evidenced by the **long stems in *t*'s and *d*'s going upward.**
- A smooth operator is shown by the **fluidity of the script.**

I'm here for sexual assault of a woman

Remember, don't be fooled by a neat and careful script. Good penmanship doesn't always represent a good person. Many people feel anxious about showing me their handwriting when they meet me because their handwriting is illegible. Remember, illegibility has nothing to do with integrity; it is more indicative of the speed of the person's mind.

To Have and to Hold

LOVE HAS NO boundaries. Love is pure. True love does not discriminate by age, race, or gender. Despite the endless news we hear of broken marriages and infidelity, here are twenty couples whose love and commitment have survived the test of time.

Research shows that 60 percent of marriages fail within the first seven years. Many wait much too late before they seek help. How couples communicate and create an understanding between each other is important. The major struggle between couples can come from:

· One partner wanting to have more control or power
· A lack of care or respect for the other partner
· A lack of interest in each other's career and goals
· Money problems
· A lack of attention or of time to play makes Jack or Jill a dull boy or girl
· Inflexibility

· External influences—e.g., drinking, drugs, gambling, in-laws

This hour was the most challenging to prepare. It was often difficult to get both partners to agree to participate: one partner would be willing and the other needed much persuasion. To all the couples who have generously participated with their handwriting samples, I am greatly appreciative. Many were even brave enough to be published under their given names.

A compatibility analysis is one of the hardest for me to prepare. First, there are three reports to prepare, one for each party and a joint report that suggests what they can both bring to the relationship. It is not the graphologist's role to give advice or make choices. We simply give all the facts to both partners and each makes a decision based on the information provided. To give advice takes away from the objectivity of the analysis.

It is often quite disheartening to give bad news to a person deeply in love. Often the client may refuse to believe and accept the information, hoping that the analysis could somehow be inaccurate. I was so anxious when I was waiting for my own to be returned.

Although I am familiar with some of these couples, I have not been part of the analysis process in their union. A few were married before I was born. Because this is a delicate area, I have concentrated on two main aspects of their personalities: their emotions and how they communicate. I have also identified one or two traits that have helped them keep their union intact. Let's look at what makes them tick.

CELEBRATING 64 YEARS

Name:	Elizabeth Abrahams (Bessie)	Henry Abrahams
Heritage:	British	British
Occupation:	Retired store owner	Retired engraver
Children:	None	

ELIZABETH (BESSIE)

She is methodical in her approach to solving problems, expressed in the **roundness of her *m*'s and *n*'s.** Her sympathetic nature is shown by the **slight slant** to the right. Her organizational strengths are shown in her **balanced *f*'s.** She speaks directly, with candor, expressed by her **closed *o*'s and *a*'s.**

With all my love to Beverley and Dear Winnie from:- Bessie xx xx

HENRY

He is a logical man, as expressed by the **vertical slant** in his script. He has a good memory, expressed by the **size of his script.** He is an analytical thinker, shown by the **v-shaped *m*'s and *n*'s.** He can be a little impatient at times, revealed by the **t bars not touching their stems.** His self-reliance is shown by the **underscore under his name.** He is quite a talker, **expressed by his open *o*'s and *a*'s.** However, in spite of their long and happy life together, Henry feels both he and Bessie have passed their "sell-by date."

It has been six years since we've seen Prev + her little boy + now we had the great pleasure of seeing them to-night + "D" is now grown into such a lovely boy, his ambition is to be president of U.S.A.

With all our Love

Auntie Bessie + Uncle Henry

CELEBRATING 55 YEARS

Name:	Charles Saunders, Sr.	Margaret Saunders
Heritage:	American	American
Occupation:	Retired Navy officer	Retired Navy nurse
Children:	1 son, 3 daughters	

CHARLES (CHUCK)

Right slants express that he is ruled by his emotions. The **balanced *f*'s** show his organizational ability. Hesitation in decision making, shown by the **small dots at the beginning of some letters** (e.g., *were*, first line, *they*, beginning of fourth line, *singing*, fifth line). **Small size** of the writing expresses his modesty. His **closed *o*'s and *a*'s** suggest he speaks with candor. A need for attention and recognition are evident by **high final endings** in the words such as *Stones, turned,*

The Rolling Stones were turned down when they applied to perform in Russia in 1967. Last week they finally got satisfaction, singing for 70,000 fans in Moscow.

M A R G A R E T (M A G G I E)

A **right slant** shows that she has a sympathetic nature. **Long
y and g tails** suggest determination, drive, and energy. **Slender loops in the g's and y's** express that she is selective with
friendships. **Long tail endings going upward** in words
such as *down* and *when* in the first line represent a generous
spirit. **Loops on the right side of her o's and a's** show she
is secretive. **Hooks at the beginning of her words** suggest
she is a collector of things. Her **balanced f's** shows she is well
organized.

*The Rolling Stones were turned down when
they applied to perform in Russia in 1967. Last
week they finally got satisfaction, singing for
70,000 fans in Moscow.*

C E L E B R A T I N G   5 1   Y E A R S

Name:	Padmini Patkah	Raj Patkah
Heritage:	Indian	Indian
Occupation:	Doctor	Lawyer
Children:	3 sons, 1 daughter	

P A D M I N I

She is very protective and nurturing, expressed by the
rounded a's (look at her *a's* in *analysis, although,* and *agreed*).
Her objective nature is expressed in the **slant of her script.**
She is independent, shown by the **small t stems.** She is a

perfectionist, **shown by her carefully placed *t* bars, even spacing between words and letters, and straight baseline.** Methodical, she takes a careful step-by-step approach to learning, indicated in her **rounded *m*'s.** She is a woman of few words, evident by her **closed *a*'s and *o*'s.** The **small size** of her handwriting shows she is well suited to work requiring concentration and attention to detail.

up now I have been waiting here and wondering for this analysis thing and although I knew said content was unimportant, I have still agonized no matter and I will just sit down and do it!

R A J

Emotionally, he is very responsive to others, as expressed by the **right slant** in his script. He speaks in a direct manner, evident by the **clean, clear *o*'s and *a*'s.** He is flexible, shown by the **bounce in his script.** He has an excellent memory, never forgets a birthday or an anniversary, as shown by the **size of his script.** He needs his space; do not crowd him. This is shown by the **space between his words.**

Everyday diffrent Software has been introduced to owners. which one is Perf no one knows until you try

CELEBRATING 47 YEARS

Name:	Victor Silenas	Ane Silenas
Heritage:	Lithuanian	Lithuanian
Occupation:	Retired mechanical engineer	Retired caregiver for Social Services
Children:	2 sons, 2 daughters	

VICTOR

He is a tenacious individual, revealed in the **hooks at the end of the *t*'s.** He is quick to reach out to others, as shown by the **right slant** of his writing. His persistence is evident in the **knots in his *t*'s,** especially in the words *portrait, painted,* and *northern.* Clarity of thought is seen by the **clear spacing between each line.** He can be secretive, shown by the **loops on the right of his *o*'s.** He may not always reveal everything. The **breaks between his letters** show that he also has a good intuitive sense.

The Unknown Painter.
The beauty of those eyes, their sadness, has come alive in my portrait. I painted you as a northern Madonna I watched you cry for your stillborn child. I remember your sudden smile. I watched your endless waiting for messages from the King....

A N E

She is able to keep her emotions under control, as shown by her **vertical slant.** She is modest, expressed by the **size of her script.** She sets high goals for herself; this is revealed by the *t* **bars crossed high.** She is a woman of few words, indicated by the **closed *o*'s and *a*'s.** Her intuition gives her almost immediate insights, and is expressed in the **gaps in her words.** Her probing mind is constantly seeking new information, as shown by the **pointed tops of her *m*'s and *n*'s.**

A few words about addressing people politely, using "jus" or "tu". The strangers, the people in authority, any body in high esteem must be addressed with "jus". The friends, family members, the children are addressed with "tu". "Tu" is warmer, closer, friendlier. "Jus" is more respectful, but also more distant, cold, unfeeling.

Some other strange sounding pronouns are: "toks, si toks" - such, of this kind, "anoks" - of that kind, "kitoks" - of a different kind, "visoks" - of all kinds, diverse, "joks" - none, not one.

How about that?

CELEBRATING 40 YEARS

Name:	Ness Shirley	Roy Shirley
Heritage:	Scottish	Scottish
Occupation:	Retired graphologist	Retired chief executive of European head-hunting company
Children:	2 daughters, 1 son	

N E S S

She is quick to show her feelings, as expressed by the **right slant of her script.** She doesn't hold back when giving to others—her generous nature often gets her into trouble—as expressed by a tendency toward **wide spacing between her letters.** Her organizational ability is expressed by her **balanced *f*'s**; she can achieve a lot. She is an open communicator, indicated by the **open *o*'s** in her script. She takes a direct and efficient approach to projects, indicated by **lack of a lead in strokes. Precisely placed *i* dots** show she is a careful and accurate person. The **form of her personal pronoun *I*** shows she is independent.

Roy's writing is as big a challenge as Roy! His pressure is strong (I know it doesn't show in the fax mode). I am so happy about your book & I cannot wait to have a copy in my hand. I would love to host a launch — keep me posted.

Best love

Ness

R o y

He feels a strong pull from his emotions and is affected by emotional experience for a long time, as expressed by his **right slant and strong pressure.** He is highly energetic, as shown by the **pressure of his script.** He can become impatient with those who can't keep up with his pace, shown by some *t* **bars on the right of the stem.** He loves action and variety, as is evident by his **long and wide lower loops.** His optimism is expressed by the **upward *t* bars and the ascending baseline.** Roy is self-reliant, which is shown by his **underscored signature.**

Ten lines, says Nessie — that used to be a school punishment! (I've just gone back and dotted all my i's !! and my exclamation marks ;; Trouble is I know so much about the grand activity of handwriting analysis — but you really can't cheat! (I'm trying like hell to get some rhythm into this and cut out my starting strokes. Sorry if you're going to use this in a book; I'm only kidding !!

Roy

CELEBRATING 40 YEARS

Name:	Alvenia Madera	Carl Madera
Heritage:	American	American
Occupation:	Homemaker	Retired electrical engineer
Children:	5 sons, 2 daughters	

ALVENIA

That she often stretches herself too thin is indicated by the **overextension of letters** into the next line (with seven children it is not surprising). She has a tendency to worry more than is necessary, shown by the **loops in her m's.** Her emotions are easily triggered, as indicated in the **forward slant** of her script. A desire for responsibility is evident in the **large circles at the beginning of her last name and in the word *your*** (second sentence, second word). She gets restless, indicated by the **loops in her p's.** Your secrets are safe with her, evident in the **loops on the right side of her o's and a's.** Strong willpower is indicated by **heavy pressure on her t bars.** She relies on logic rather than intuition, as shown by her **highly connected writing.** That Alvenia is careful and methodical about decision making is evident in her **rounded m's and n's.**

I have enjoyed meeting you and being in your company. Your family and friends are so fortunate to have you as their own. So many interesting times you have experienced. I could only wish to be able to see you at a later time to catch up on all you have been doing.

Alvenia E. Madera

CARL

He is a romantic idealist, expressed by the **height of the upper-zone letters,** especially his *l*'s and *t*'s. He sets practical goals for himself, expressed in the *t* **bars crossed in the middle of the stem.** He is organized, shown in his **balanced *f*'s.** His emotions are readily stirred, as shown by the **right slant** of the script. He expresses himself with candor, evident in **his closed *o*'s and *a*'s.** His **legible signature** with his name in full shows he has no hidden agenda. He is a family man, as expressed by the **equal size of the capital *c* and *m*.** The **bounce** in his script shows he can accommodate last-minute changes. **Curved final strokes** show his generosity. His **long *t* bars** show he brings much enthusiasm to his family.

Hope you stay for a long time in the Program. You will enjoy and benefit from doing so.

A new friend,

Carl A. Madera (Andy)

CELEBRATING 39 YEARS

Name:	Kathryn Duncan	Peter Duncan
Heritage:	English/ American Indian	Polish
Occupation:	Senior receptionist	Retired police officer
Children:	2 daughters, 1 son	

KATHRYN

She has a highly responsive nature, evident in the **right slant,** and her generous nature is shown by the **wide spacing between her letters.** She is modest and quite happy staying in the background, shown by the **size of her script.** She is strong willed, evident in the **strong *t* bars,** and can hold her ground by being stubborn, evident in the *t*'s **with two stems.** An open communicator, she is ready to express her feelings, shown by the **open *a*'s and *o*'s.**

My children are the joy in my life and when the Grandchildren came along I was so pleased I knew that it doesn't get better than this. In five years my two oldest daughters gave us four Grandchildren, 2 Boys and 2 Girls. Each are very different and unik. I cried at each birth as I was so overwhelmed

PETER

That he is a man of high morals is evident in the **height of the upward letters such as *l*, *h*, and *t*.** He is often spontaneous—his **right slant** expresses this. **Heavy pressure and big lower loops** show he is energetic and likes to socialize and try new activities. His sociability may vary—some of his ***g*'s are looped**—but he also enjoys quiet time alone, indicated by the **straight downstrokes in the *y*'s.** A few hidden **loops in his *w*'s** suggest that he is a worrier. He is willing to share his thoughts and ideas, expressed by the **open *o*'s and *a*'s.** The **loops in the *l*'s** express his imagination. He is an idea person. His enthusiasm is contagious, as shown by his **long *t* bars.**

CELEBRATED 38 YEARS

Name:	Barbara Golden	Edwin Robert Golden
Heritage:	African American	African American
Occupation:	Teacher	President of health-care company
Children:	5 daughters	

BARBARA

What you see is what you get—evident in her spontaneous, **legible script.** Her generosity is shown by the **spacing between her letters** and her **curved final strokes.** She engages in positive self-affirmation, and her optimism is shown by her **rising baseline** and the *t* **bars crossed high.** The **right slant** of her script shows she is ruled by her heart.

That she is an open communicator is evident in her **open *o*'s and *a*'s,** and her humor is expressed by the **initial wavy lines in her capital *m*'s and *n*'s** (in the last line).

Tired and worn out, but today was fun and worth the work! It's hard to believe that in less than two weeks Nugget will be Mrs. Nugget Mitchell. I'll miss her.

Barbara P. Golden

B O B

His signature shows that he was ruled by his heart, expressed by the **slant** in his script. Both letters of his **first and last name are equally the same size**—family and self were equally important to him. The **Greek** *e* expresses his love for literature, and the **wide upper and lower loops** are evidence of a good imagination. The **loop on the right side of the** *o* shows he was a good confidant; a secret was safe with him. The **retraced** *d* expresses dignity.

This hour is dedicated to Mr. Edwin Golden, who lost his battle to cancer while I was preparing this book. He left this earth on June 24, 1997. We celebrate his memory and his wonderful spirit.

CELEBRATING 35 YEARS

Name:	Potenciana Chan	Nicolas M. Chan
Heritage:	Filipino	Filipino
Occupation:	Clerical assistant	Retired embassy driver
Children:	3 daughters, 4 sons	

NICOLAS

His **vertical slant** shows he is a logical man who has no trouble staying calm in a crisis. Don't crowd him; he needs his space. This is expressed by the **wide space between each word.** He has good self-control—the **bowed *t* bars** express this. He does not readily reveal personal information, indicated by the **loops on the right side of his *a*'s.** The **size of his script** shows he sees the big picture.

*i am pleased to be a part
of this, and I hope this will
help you what u need.
            Good luck!
                —Nicolas M. Chan*

POTENCIANA

Whereas Nicolas welcomes distractions (expressed in his **large script**), Potenciana stays focused, shown in the **smaller size** of her script. She is quick to respond to emotion, indicated by the **right slant.** Willing to accommodate the needs of others, she is flexible, shown by the **bounce in her script.** Although friendly, she is very selective when choosing her friends, expressed in the **slender *y*'s.** She can be a little stubborn at times, indicated by **two stems in her *t*'s.** Her **curved final strokes** show her to be caring and generous. Whereas Nicolas sees the big picture, Potenciana is able to focus on the daily nitty-gritty details, as shown by the ***i* dots close to the stem.**

It's my pleasure to be publish in your Book. I'm proud to be a Filipino and at the same time to be an American

Potenciana Chan

CELEBRATING 34 YEARS

Name:	Jan Bors	Philippa Bors
Heritage:	Dutch	Dominican
Occupation:	Sales executive	Homemaker
Children:	2 daughters	

JAN

He does not like to draw attention to himself; he is very modest, expressed by the **size of his script.** His sympathetic nature is indicated by the **semi-right slant** of his script. He is ambitious, setting high goals for himself, as is expressed by the *t* **bars crossed at the top of the stems.** He is independent, indicated by **no stems on his *d*'s.** Effective time management is expressed by the efficient use of **space and amount of words on a line.** He is direct in his communication with others, expressed by his **closed *o*'s and *a*'s.** His **pressure** shows good physical stamina. His **large lower loops** show his desire for social interaction.

Our girls are grown up now. Debbi is a successful fashion designer and has made us grandparents for the first time recently. Desiree is a merchandise manager in the growing credit industry and looking to buy her first flat. We are all well and grateful that life has been good for us so far... Sorry for the delay in writing but then, better late than never! Best wishes and regards from all of us

Jenni. *Jan*

P HILIPPA

Her reserved nature is expressed by her **backward slant.**
Her **upward *t* bars** show that she is an optimist. Her **spacing of letters** in her words indicates her intuitiveness; she
often goes by her gut feeling. A lot can go unsaid between her
and Jan. She speaks only when she has something worth saying, indicated by her **closed *o*'s.** Her **large *k* buckle** shows
she does not want others telling her what to do. She is independent. Her **simplified letters with no lead strokes** tell
you she is direct and straightforward.

Just a few lines as promised. I
was wonderful seeing you all
last night. The arranged surprise
visit for Mum was fun.
Digby has really grown and he
is very polite. You are doing
a fantastic job as a mother.
Keep it up!!
We are very happy for you, and
therefore would like to wish you
good luck with your book
and other future plans.
Love
Philippa

CELEBRATING 29 YEARS

Name:	Delores Hodges	Rev. Robert Hodges
Heritage:	African American	African American
Occupation:	Credit manager	Minister
Children:	3 sons	

REV. ROBERT HODGES

He lives by his own internal code of values, as shown by the **upper letters such as *l*, *t*, and *d* extending high.** He plans his work by setting practical goals, expressed by the **height of his *t* bars.** His determination and drive are shown in his *g*'s and *y*'s. His **open *e*'s** indicate he is a good listener. His **right slant** expresses a natural understanding and interest in others. His **open *o*'s express** his ability to communicate well. The **equal size of the initials** in his name express that he is a family man. **Wedged *m*'s and *n*'s** show an analytical mind. His **rising baseline** shows his optimism.

Bless the Lord O my soul and forget not all His benefits

Robert L. Hodges

DELORES

She is sensitive to others' needs, as expressed by the **forward slant** of her writing. Her generosity is seen in her **wide letterspacing and curved final strokes.** When she's in an unfamiliar situation, you can depend on her to think on her feet, evident in the **figure-eight *g*'s** in her signature. She communicates with candor, as expressed by her clear **o's and a's.** Her **wide spacing between words** shows her independence.

Oh, taste and see that the Lord is good and his mercy endureth forever.

CELEBRATING 26 YEARS

Name:	Margo L. Williams	Cheryl D. Reese
Heritage:	African American	African American
Occupation:	Psychoeducational therapist	Health educator
Children:	None	

M A R G O

Her emotions influence her decision-making process, as expressed by the **slant of her writing.** Her need to acquire is expressed by the **hooks at the beginning of some of her letters.** She needs her own space, evident by the **spacing between her words.** She speaks when she has something important to say, shown by her **closed *o*'s and *a*'s.** The **initial curve in the *M* in *Margo*** shows she has a sense of humor. **Regularity in size and layout** expresses her liking for a structured and predictable environment. **Hooks at the ends** of her letters show that she is tenacious when it comes to holding on to things, especially ideas she has acquired.

Today has all kind of surprises, I have watched people sell their products with excitement and joy. I too, love the world I have co-created.

Margo A. Williams

CHERYL

She has a sympathetic heart, shown by her **slant.** She is organized, shown by her **balanced f's.** She is frank and direct, evident by her **closed o's and a's.** She is a loyal friend and partner, shown by the **clear i dots over the stems.** She sets high goals for herself, **evident in the t bars crossed high.** Like Margo, the regularity in form and space is evident of her desire for structure. The **upward slant of her t bars** shows she keeps a positive outlook. Some **t and d stems are very short,** expressing independent thinking.

Life is exciting for me and I do not believe that I would have the same experience if I had not shared it with Margo.

Cheryl D. Reese

CELEBRATING 25 YEARS

Name:	Karin Merritt	Melvin Merritt
Heritage:	German	African American
Occupation:	Nurse	Military budget manager
Children:	1 daughter	

MELVIN

He can blend in or stand out, depending upon the circumstances, evident by the **spacing between his words.** A clear approach to handling problems is expressed by the **clear spacing between each line.** He does not let emotions interfere with his judgment, as indicated by the **vertical slant.** He likes his own company and doesn't need to be one of the boys, as expressed by the **straight *y*'s. Wide word spacing** shows he needs space. You can rely on him to be **frank and direct,** shown by his clear ***o*'s and *a*'s.** He treads carefully; caution is shown by the **straight line at the end of his letter *s*.** The **small size of his script** shows he concentrates well. He can be a little stubborn at times, shown by the **wedged *t* stems.**

> By the way a vacation
> in Jamaica sounds great. Let me/us
> know more about places to go there
> I hope this is enough.
>
> See Ya
> Mel

KARIN

Fluidity in her script—for example, the way her *f*'s and *g*'s **flow into the next letter**—expresses flexibility. Her **right slant** suggests her emotions are easily stirred. The **slender loops in her *g*'s and *y*'s** show she is selective in her friendships with others. She is intuitive and often makes a decision based on what seems her sixth sense, indicated by the **spacing between her words.** Stubbornness is indicated by the *t* **written with a triangle on the left.** She speaks only when she has something to say, expressed by her **closed *o*'s and *a*'s.** **Light pressure** shows Karin is a gentle person who is given to forgive and forget.

Her **even spacing of letters, words, and lines** show she has a clear perspective and is naturally well organized.

My drive to work is about 4 miles.
I have to pass through one village, where the
street curves several times.
A good portion of the road I am travelling
on, is lined by vineyards and orchards.
This region is famous for its mild climate
and abundance of produce and wine
grown here.

Karin Herott

CELEBRATING 25 YEARS

Name:	Jeong Hee Kwon	O Kyung Kwon
Heritage:	South Korean	South Korean
Occupation:	Clothing store owner	Research engineer
Children:	2 sons	

JEONG HEE KWON

She sets practical goals for herself, expressed by the *t* **bars crossed in the middle of the stem.** She is sympathetic, expressed by the **slight slant of her script.** The **size of her script** expresses her modest nature. She is a woman of few words; her **closed** *a***'s and** *o***'s** express this. Her acquisitiveness, shown in her **initial hook on the letter** *s* (look at the words *slippy, sloppy*), makes her a keen businesswoman. **Carefully placed** *i* **dots** show attention to detail and accuracy. Her **letterspacing and curved final strokes** show she likes to share with others. Her **retraced** *t***'s and** *d***'s** are evidence of dignity and poise.

Once upon a time there was a frog called Mr. Jeremy Fisher ; he lived in a little damp house amongst the buttercups at the edge of a pond. The water was all slippy - sloppy in the larder

O KYUNG KWON

His slant expresses a sympathetic nature and the **straight *y*'s** represent that he likes time alone. He sets high goals for himself, evident in the **high-crossed *t* bars.** He is a handyman, expressed by the **flat-roof *r*'s.** His **open *b*'s** represent his business acumen. He can think fast in a crisis, expressed by **figure-eight *g*'s.** He will be direct in his communication, expressed by his **closed, clean *o*'s and *a*'s.** The **size of his script** is evidence of good concentration and memory. His **even spacing of words, letters, and lines** shows he is well organized.

Unlike most books on the object-oriented technology, this book is written for managers, not engineers. I've kept the technical details to a minimum and introduced jargon only as necessary to explain the technology. I don't assume that you know how to program a computer or even use one, but I do assume that you are generally familiar with computers and how they are used in business.

CELEBRATING 21 YEARS

Name:	Jackie Scott-Walker	Martin Walker
Heritage:	Guyanese	Guyanese
Occupation:	Teacher	Entrepreneur
Children:	2 daughters, 2 sons	

JACKIE

She has a sympathetic ear for everyone, expressed by her **forward slant.** Her **open *e*'s** show she is a good listener. **Light**

pressure shows she is a gentle person. She is an analytical thinker, a "why person"—you better have all the facts before you present your case—indicated by the **v-shaped n's, m's, and h's.** She is open in her communication, expressed by her **open a's and o's.** The **simplicity of her script** shows she is a bottom-line thinker. What may seem complicated to others, Jackie will find a way to simplify.

> *Hopefully, this will be O.K.!*
> *He couldn't think of anything*
> *else to write — if you need more*
> *than this, let me know.*

MARTIN

He is spontaneous and strongly influenced by his emotions, expressed by his **forward right slant.** An independent person, he has **short d stems.** He welcomes distractions, evident by the **large script.** Don't push him if he says no—he's stubborn, expressed by the **two stems in t bars. Heavy pressure** indicates high physical endurance. His **strong t bars** show he has strong willpower. His **pointed m's and n's** show he is an analytical thinker. He needs to know why. His **closed o's and a's** show he is very careful in what he reveals about himself.

> *The Cat Jumped over the moon*
> *The big fat cat sat on the mat*
> *M.*

CELEBRATING 19 YEARS

Name:	Jean Tomlin Russell	Frank Russell
Heritage:	Jamaican	Jamaican
Occupation:	Human resources director	Consultant for a charity
Children:	1 son, 1 daughter	

J E A N

She is ruled by her head, **shown by her vertical script.** She is a practical person, expressed by her *t* **bars crossed in the middle.** She is tenacious and determined, evidenced by the **hooks at the ends of her long downstrokes,** e.g., *y*'s. Optimism is expressed by her **ascending *t* bars.** She is willing to share her opinions and is direct and open in her communication, as suggested by her **open *o*'s and *a*'s.** Independence is shown by her **straight personal pronoun *I*.** Analytical thinking is evident by her **v-shaped *m*'s and *n*'s.**

living in Jeans and duffle coats. It just doesn't seem like me, I suppose it's because I'm getting older + am settling down.
Anyway Bev sorry this letter is so short but I have a book review to write now, so take care + get well soon.

lots of love

Jean xxxx

FRANK

He is a practical man, expressed by the *t*'s **crossed in the middle of the stems.** His **heavy pressure** shows energy and a sensuous nature. He speaks with candor, as shown in his **closed *o*'s and *a*'s.** He is sincere and loyal—look closely at how he **dots his *i*'s clear and clean.** His clarity of thought is evident in the **spacing between his lines.** He is a fluid thinker, expressed in his *t*'s **running through to connect with the *h*'s.** He is determined, indicated by the **length of his *g*'s and *y*'s.**

Sorry for the delay, quick note as promised,
Jean, Nzinga and Ndeh all send their love
and are really happy about your successes.
We look forward to a copy when it comes
out.

CELEBRATING 12 YEARS ★

Name:	Danny Dacosta	Geneva Dacosta
Heritage:	Jamaican	Grenadian
Occupation:	Photographer/ business owner	Business partner in a photographic studio
Children:	3 daughters	

★This couple have been united for thirty years. After eighteen years together, they tied the knot.

DANNY

He has high energy, expressed by the **lengthy *y*'s** in his script. He can think on his feet, expressed by his **figure-eight's.** Look at the *s* in the word *stand* in the first sentence and *session* and *studio* in the last sentence. His enthusiasm is expressed by his **sweeping t's.** His tenacity is expressed by **hooks at the ends of the letters,** such as the *g*'s in the first two sentences. He is very open about expressing his emotions, indicated by his **right slant.** You can trust him with your secrets, expressed by the **loops on the right in his *o*'s.** His **tall upper and long lower loops** show good imagination. The **speed** with which his writing seems to run across the page indicates the speed of his thinking and actions (fast). The **tangling of his letters** between lines shows he may feel spread too thin by being involved in too many projects.

GENEVA

A **vertical slant** suggests she is able to maintain objectivity and get all the facts before taking action. She sets practical goals, expressed by the *t* **bars crossed in the middle of the stems.** Her spirituality is shown by the height of **upper letters such as *l*'s and *t*'s.** She will be candid in her communication with you, indicated by the **clean, closed *a*'s and *o*'s.** The **figure-eight formation in her *g*'s and *s*'s** in the words *girls, seeing,* and *wishing* suggest a creative and fluid mind. The **large size and width of her letters** show she presents herself with confidence. Flexible communication skills are indicated by her **open *e*'s,** which show she is a good listener. Her strong intuition gives her keen awareness of people and situations around her, expressed through the **spacing in her words.**

Any way next time as The girls
were very keen to come. I suspect
they had ulterior motive.

Wishing you very best with your
book and The tour.

Look forward to seeing you both/three
next time.

Love Geneva

CELEBRATING 12 YEARS

Name:	Daniel Miller	Michael Matthews
Heritage:	American	American
Occupation:	Musician	Music teacher, singer
Children:	None	

DANIEL

His creative ability is expressed in his **looped *l*'s and *f*'s.** The **large upper loops** show imagination, which he uses to write and create original pieces. His modest nature is evident by the **small size of the script.** He digs his heels in if he doesn't want to do something, expressed by his ***t*'s shaped like a star.** The **bounce in his script** expresses his flexibility. His sympathetic nature is expressed by his **slant.** He is secretive, shown in the **loops on the right of his *a*'s and *o*'s. Heavy pressure** as seen by **small pools of ink** in some of the loops and ovals indicates a sensuous nature. In his case we know it is an appreciation of music. His **pointed *m*'s and *n*'s** show his ability to analyze, useful in understanding music theory.

I am choosing to write about some of my activities and hobbies. I am a symphony musician. The double bass is my instrument. I have been playing in the Houston Symphony for 20 years. I received my Bachelors and Masters of Music from Rice University's Shepherd School of Music.

MICHAEL

He is considerate of others, indicated by the **slant** of his script. Although intuitive, he may not always listen to his sixth sense, expressed by the **space in his words.** He is a long-term planner, evident in his **_t_ bars crossed high.** He is a conflict avoider, evident in his **closed _o_'s and _a_'s.** His **small, simplified writing** indicates good technical abilities. The **lower loops, which are large** in comparison with the rest of his writing, indicate a love of activity and variety. A **flexible baseline** reflects his adaptability. The **wedged _t_ stems** show he can be strong-willed and may not yield. His **efficient use of space** reflects his efficient use of time. He also has **small pools of ink** in his loops and ovals, suggesting a sensuous nature.

CELEBRATING 8 YEARS

Name:	Pasha Kincaid	Kofi Kincaid
Heritage:	South African	Ghanaian
Occupation:	Storyteller/artist	Mailman
Children:	2 daughters	

PASHA

The **gaps in her words** express her strong intuition, which gives her keen perception. When she has something to say, she will not mix her words but be direct, expressed by her **clean, clear o's and a's.** Clarity of thought and an ability to get to the bottom line are expressed by the **simplicity of her letters.** A need for variety is important to Pasha, evident in the **long tails in her g's and y's.** Self-reliance is shown by the **underscore below her signature.** An interest in others is shown by the **slant** in her script. Her flexibility is shown in her **bouncy baseline.** Her **unique letterforms** indicate creativity.

Hidden in the innocent mind and spirit of the child are talents and maybe even genius for goodness.
Education is the key for releasing this infinite resource
Education brings out this innate goodness and develops it.

Pasha Kincaid

KOFI

That he is a practical and logical man is expressed by his **vertical strokes.** He has a good eye for detail—his *i* **dots are close to the stems.** Don't crowd him—he needs his space, as the **spacing between words** suggests (look especially at the last two lines). He is a good listener, revealed by his **open *e*'s,** and willing to talk, evident in his **open *o*'s and *a*'s.** A direct approach to life and a clear perspective are evident in the **simple formation of his letters. Rounded *m*'s and *n*'s** show a careful approach in planning and decision making. **Regularity in his writing** indicates he likes an orderly environment.

Blessings on the Blossom

Blessings on the fruit

Blessings on the leaf and stem

and Blessings on the Root

and Blessings on the Meal

CELEBRATING 8 YEARS

Name:	Lee Lumbley	Jeff Ganz
Heritage:	American	American
Occupation:	Musician	Entrepreneur
Children:	None	

LEE

He is a creative individual, expressed by his **flat-roof r's.** He is kind and sympathetic, evident in the **slight slant** in his script. He is a fluid thinker, expressed by the way **each stroke glides into the next.** Optimism is shown by the **ascending baseline and upward t bars.** A collector is expressed in the **hooks at the beginning of his letters.**

Last weekend, my companion and I travelled to New York City. We went to see a specific person in a play.

We arrived on Friday evening and had dinner with the friend with whom we stayed.

On Saturday, we rose early and walked from her house to Union Square. She lives at W 55th and 10th Avenue. We stopped every three or four blocks and shopped or knoshed. Since it was hot out, the air-conditioning in the stores, the iced coffee's, or the gelatti offered us relief. We returned to our friends' home, caught up on the news of the day, and dressed for dinner. After dinner, we headed to the theatre.

Lee Lumbley   .

JEFF

He is the nurturing type, expressed by his **covered-top *a*'s.**
He has a good memory, shown by the **size of his script.** He
is practical and logical, shown by his **vertical strokes.** He is
clear thinking, evidenced by the **spacing between lines.**
Optimism and flexibility are suggested by the **ascending
baseline and upward *t* bars.** A literary type, he has
rounded *d* stems.

Dear Beverly,

I am so excited and honored to be a part of this fascinating project. This book sounds great! And what a wonderful opportunity for you. I hope it turns out to be everything you want.

Everybody I tell about this is so jealous. They all want to have thier handwriting analyzed. I told them all to wait for the book and buy it.

Thanks again for this opportunity. I hope to see you soon.

There is much diversity in the writing of the couples we have looked at. What they have in common are many positive traits, such as responsiveness to others, flexibility, humor, good listening skills, self-reliance, readiness to express feelings, and interest in new experiences. These are all qualities that can only enhance a relationship.

If you look closely at all the profiles of the men, you will see a consistent pattern in most of them. Many of their partners have the opposite temperament, except for Mr. and Mrs. Kwon, who have the same temperament. But in most cases, one partner leads and the other has the reins on his or her emotions. Many of these couples felt that they were not compatible, but had over the years worked through their challenges with understanding, communication, patience, and love. At the same time, the couples also had in common the absence of numerous negative traits, such as selfishness, dominance, aggression, anger, compulsive lying, instability—all qualities that would tear down a relationship.

We are all a mixture of both positive and negative personality traits. Many times our negative traits develop as defenses against perceived threats to our ego. With understanding from others and hard work on our part, we may be able to overcome the traits that make us difficult. It is a fact that when we see an accumulation of these negative traits in a potential partner, we can be sure we are on the road to a toxic and unhealthy relationship.

The dynamics of personal interactions are far too complex to be neatly categorized in this section. Therefore, there are no specific formulas that promise or can guarantee success in any relationship. Over a period of time, each couple has faced different obstacles and challenges that have strengthened their relationship.

So maybe you have already found that someone special. If you think it was hard finding him, it is much harder keeping your relationship with him healthy and happy, at a level where you are both comfortable, maintaining your lifestyles, careers, and self-esteem. Many couples stay married for various reasons—children, finances, convenience—but to be happily married and able to exist within a relationship is a task by itself. A mixture of the following is much needed: trust, patience, balance, understanding, commitment, being each other's cheerleader, the ability to compromise without sabotaging yourself, some similarities of interest, being united but holding on to your own identity, recognizing each other's strengths, having some similar temperament qualities and value systems.

Apart from being generous with their handwriting samples, the women in our couples wanted to share some of their wisdom about staying married. Here are twenty tips:

1. Keep an element of surprise in your relationship.
2. Don't get so caught up in the wedding plans that you forget you are going to spend the rest of your life with this person.
3. Marry someone who shows an interest in your goals and dreams.
4. Marry a man for what he is, not for his potential.
5. Marry a man that trusts your judgment.
6. Excite him; be sexually creative and imaginative.
7. Let some things go—don't make a big deal about everything—but don't become a pushover either.
8. Talk about everything—money, children, sex, careers. If there are things you can't talk about, the longer you leave these issues unresolved, the more they will bother you.

9. Whatever the man's rules are about money, have your own—be independent.

10. Don't let yourself go with calories, clothes, and children. *Be the other woman.* He may fuss about how much it all costs, but when someone else tells him how great his wife looks, he'll love it.

11. Expect nothing but get everything. Expectations are about waiting. When you and your partner have too many expectations, you sometimes end up just waiting for things to happen. Get busy and create your goals and dreams together.

12. Do not lose your own identity for the sake of a relationship, but be ready to compromise at times and continue to work on the relationship. A good one doesn't just happen but grows slowly.

13. Give each other space; don't stop having friends and doing things for yourself or by yourself.

14. Don't go to bed angry with each other. Don't part company angry either.

15. Don't make a point to mention all the irritating things he does that bother you.

16. To say nothing can be helpful to avoid an argument, especially if you know in your heart you are right. Just smile and keep walking.

17. Look at your partner as a blossoming flower. Count his petals and not his thorns.

18. Keep only passion in the bedroom—reduce the headache excuses.

19. Know the scents that your partner likes and stick to them, the ones that lure him closer to you.

20. Develop a fondness and admiration system. Let go of past issues. Stay focused on the issue at hand and find a solution, rather than continue to accuse and blame.

As one of the women from this hour advised me, couples should focus on communication, how to resolve conflict, and commitment to their vows. Marriage is like the weather: there are days when it is sunny and you are carefree, and days when it is gray and cloudy—and sometimes the storm comes and lasts for more than a few weeks. You just have to find ways to weather the storm. Don't jump ship, but hold on tightly to each other.

At the Stroke of . . .

Twelve

The Single Girl's Guide

THE MIDNIGHT HOUR is here again and your prince didn't come—another night alone. As little girls we are socialized to believe that our prince or knight in shining armor will come and sweep us off our feet. That's what the storybooks told us. Well, they lied. The pressure becomes more intense the older we get. So there is a mad race to get to the finish line. Our biological clocks are ticking, we are walking time bombs. I was at a conference earlier this year and an attractive and highly intelligent woman announced that she was getting married on July 4. Everyone gathered around to congratulate her. Then she announced that she had instituted a nationwide search to find a man by that date. This is positive thinking to the extreme! I loved her sense of humor, but do we have to go to these limits?

Wake up! Stop waiting for him! If you think he's coming with a Porsche and a Cartier wedding band, think twice. You may have already met him, but through some sort of misunderstanding, one way or the other, one of you blew it. Make

a plan for your next date. Decide how you can make it different. Change your attitude and your behavior. You can adjust
your life. First clear out the clutter, the negative energy, the
anger and bitterness. When you make space, better will always
come. Clear the decks; a new ship is coming in. Be happy single. Be happy with yourself. Learn to love yourself and be in
awe of the wonderment and greatness of your unique self.
When you have achieved this, your man will be there, I guarantee you. Men know when you are desperate. They can read
you the way you think you can read them.

In my single days, I shared my home in London with several eligible, handsome bachelors (including the one I'm
married to). I got an inside view of how men behave by
my house-sharing experiences: how they respond to being
chased and what they like or do not like in a woman. They
were united in wanting an intelligent, independent woman
who had her act together and had a sense of self, someone a
little elusive who would not take too much BS from them.
Although their egos were greatly boosted by women who
chased them, it was the ones they couldn't get that aroused
their interest the most. *Ms. Elusive wins every time!*

Here are some guidelines that I learned along the way and
want to share with you. Take this path with me, step by step.

1. How do you find a good man? Stop looking! Have you ever
tried to find a phone number of an old friend you ran into a
few days ago? You turn your purse inside out looking for it.
You can't call her because you can't find the phone number.
Then one day, when you are looking for something else, there
it is, right in front of you. Well, men are the same; they show
up when they are ready, in their own good time. "Men are like
buses," my father would say. "Don't run after them. There will

always be another. There may be a wait, and it may not be the number you want, but you can be sure there *will* be another."

2. *Ms. Elusive always wins.* Don't play games, but do not always be available. Find a hobby, create other interests in your life. I answered the phone one evening at my home, and a young lady wanted to speak to my roommate. The young lady called three times before my roommate came home. He shook his head and mouthed, "Tell her I'm not home." Wouldn't you just die if you overheard this or could see his reaction if you were the caller on the other end of the line? Don't stay home by the phone. Return calls, of course, but stop chasing men and calling them. When they are ready to speak with you, they will call, and if they are lucky they will catch up with *you.*

3. *Enhance your personal power.* Continue to work on yourself all the time. We are all works in progress. Enhance your power on all levels, emotionally, spiritually, sexually (yes, sexually—know your own body and what you like before you expect your partner to please you), intellectually, and physically. Read *everything.* Expand your reading list beyond self-help books (they can provide you with a source of information but experience will always be your best teacher). Read great works such as: *One Hundred Years of Solitude,* Gabriel García Márquez; *Second-Class Citizen,* Buchi Emecheta; *Things Fall Apart,* Chinua Achebe; *The Joy Luck Club,* Amy Tan; *Jude the Obscure,* Thomas Hardy; *Dubliners,* James Joyce; *A Bridge Through Time,* Laila Abou-Saif; and *Invisible Life,* E. Lynn Harris (a *must*-read for every woman, especially young adults new to the dating game). The list is endless. Go to seminars, lectures, retreats. Continue to further your education. Embrace other cultures. Travel will be by far your best teacher always. Join or-

ganizations and professional clubs, e.g., a skiing club. The more varied and interesting things you do, the more interesting you become.

Make yourself an interesting, valuable person in your community. Reach out and touch somebody. Volunteer for a charity, or become one of Oprah's Network Angels. When you think you are at your lowest ebb, you will meet or hear of someone whose situation is worse than yours. By helping someone else, you begin to appreciate what you have, and giving of yourself will help you to forget your own problems and realize how blessed you really are. There is always someone out there in a worse situation than yourself. Help her enhance her own progress and in turn you will be rewarded in some other way.

The Power of Communication

You catch bees with honey, not lemon. Sweet words stay longer on a man's mind than sarcasm.

When you increase your knowledge, you enhance your power of oral communication. Many men find intelligence in women almost as sexy as the act itself. Your conversations should be interesting. Be direct, but do not turn your conversations into an inquisition every time you meet a man or speak on the phone. Although a large proportion of the men in my survey said the initial turn-on was sex appeal, it was the level of intelligence of a woman that kept them in the relationship longer. Remember, more is less, and less is more. Let the man's imagination run wild. Concentrate on the depth of the individual and not the superficial trappings. Degrees, cars, money, clothes are all very attractive and enticing, but look deeper. Just because the man has possessions, it doesn't mean they will be yours. Also remember *your own self-worth is higher and greater than his net worth.*

Listen with your mind and not your heart. Remember what the man tells you; pay attention all the time to every word. And watch what he does and how he does it, how he treats you and how he treats the people he says are close to him, especially his mother.

4. Learn to love yourself and know what you love. Listen to your inner voice. It guides you more than you think. Trust yourself. Once you trust your own judgment, you will trust your partner more. Learn to enjoy your own company. Make yourself happy first, because you alone are responsible for your own happiness and no one else.

Learn to be *still.* Do nothing sometimes. In this fast-paced society that we live in, it is rare that we get a chance to do nothing. There is always something to be done: watching television, listening to the radio, reading a book, meeting, greeting, visiting, caring. Just sit and be still. Enjoy the re-union with your inner self.

Allow yourself to hear your own heartbeat. It is talking to you, telling you your dreams, your passions, and your desires, but often you cannot hear it because you are rushing here and there, going to school, picking up kids, bringing work home in commitment after commitment. Just *stop,* be still, and re-unite with yourself. Be happy without a man. He enhances your existence but he doesn't and should *not* determine it. If one comes along but the relationship is not working, brush yourself off, dust yourself down, and start all over again. Many women stay in a state of unhappiness, afraid to let go, afraid they will be by themselves, afraid that this is the best that life has to offer. The best is yet to come. If something doesn't fit, do not force it. If things are not working well in the earlier months then, when the reality of children, careers, and mortgage payments has to be faced, you need some foundation to keep everything else going. *Lust is not enough.*

Learn to forgive yourself for past mistakes. Accept that you cannot change the past but can begin a new path with a new attitude and mind-set. If your relationship with your father was not ideal or nonexistent, and you hurt too much to forgive him, forgive yourself. Don't stay stuck on memories of abuse or abandonment. It will be difficult to create a relationship with another man if you have not been able to forgive the behavior of the first man in your life. If your relationship with your father has not been ideal, do not define yourself through him. Doing so will constantly hinder future relationships. Release the anger, pain, and abandonment. You cannot change the past but you can change the future.

5. *Keep your cheerleaders and forget the fear leaders.* Surround yourself with positive and supportive people. Listen to the wise and the ones who have been in committed relationships for a long time They can offer you sound advice. When I was a newlywed, my aunt, who had been married for forty-two years, suggested to me quite subtly that I was hardheaded. Me? Never! She suggested that I didn't always have to be right. Neither do you. Always trying to prove a point causes unnecessary arguments. The man already knows you are intelligent, so there is no need to constantly remind him. I did take heed. But, I must admit, every now and then I slip.

I really resent single people giving me unwanted advice on how to be married. To stay married or in a committed relationship, I recommend you take advice and lessons from those married or in committed relationships *longer* than you. Your single girlfriends will sometimes give you advice that may intentionally hinder your relationship rather than helping it. You know misery loves company.

6. *Acquire your own wealth, both spiritually and financially.* Becoming more connected spiritually makes you more deeply grounded, more trusting of yourself, more at peace with yourself. There is only one person you truly have to answer to, and you won't be marrying him! So trust the spirit, the creator. He/She won't let you down. Where you are is where you need to be right this moment because you are not ready for more. When you are ready, your mate will be there.

Save, save, save! Have a financial plan. Do you have a will? Prepare one. Do you have a retirement plan? Invest your money and understand how to make your money grow. Look at ways to increase your income. Do you know where you want to be in five years? Look at pages 208–210 to assist you in creating your five-year plan. Don't sit back waiting for Prince Charming to come and give everything to you. Remember, God blesses the child who has her own. Look at ways of getting into the property market. Make a start; invest in property. Start with an efficiency or a condo. Stop making landlords rich. Rent is money wasted, not invested. When I first moved to the United States, I often heard this expression among women, "When the going gets tough, the tough go shopping." Please stop spending what you don't have. It is counterproductive for your personal development and financial growth, and only a short-term fix. Let your credit cards work *for* you. Use them with self-control and only in an emergency, budgeting yourself within each billing cycle. Get into the habit of paying more than the minimum payment. Use credit cards that offer perks such as frequent-flyer miles, cash rewards, or other gifts. Keep your credit history clean so that when you apply for a home or business loan, there will be no disappointments. If you are brave enough to do plastic surgery, cut your credit cards up.

7. Zero tolerance to abusive behavior. Start the way you mean to continue. Do not accept lateness, rudeness, or any kind of physical or mental abuse, ever. This behavior is nonnegotiable and unacceptable. If you accept this behavior, you lose power and control. Look at abuse beyond violence. Someone who talks down to you, tries to control you, does not allow you to express yourself is abusing you. When your voice and opinions cannot be heard, you are being controlled and abused by your partner. This is unhealthy and unacceptable. If you give in at the beginning, it will be hard to make changes later. Don't accept any part of it, no matter how handsome you think the man is. This behavior makes him quite ugly. Men who beat or are abusive to women are out of control. What they are trying to achieve is power. This is not love. Love doesn't hurt like this. (See samples on pages 119-22.)

8. Have you checked out of the Heartbreak Hotel? So you got your heart broken and it hurt. Guess what? This has happened to almost every man you will meet, too. Get over it and try something different this time. Sometimes there are lessons to be learned from the frogs that we kiss. We have to kiss a few frogs to be able to recognize the prince when he comes. The frogs teach us what we do *not* want for our future. From every disappointment comes a life lesson that we can learn from. We must be wise enough not to keep on making the same mistakes again and again. If you do make the same mistakes, you have not yet learned the lesson.

Leave at the door the baggage from previous relationships. Give yourself time between relationships to clear your head, heal your heart, and get rid of the anger and pain. Forgive and forget, and move on. Do not compare your new partner with the previous one. Do not carry all your old anxieties into the next relationship. Check into your new room with a clean sheet. No one can get in if the door to your heart is closed.

9. *Men are not convenience stores, where you pick up what you want and leave.* Learn to give, because the more you give, the more you receive. Didn't your mother tell you that? There is joy in the giving. Give openly and willingly without looking for a return. The Bible says, "It is more blessed to give than to receive." It always comes back to you tenfold, in a different form. Having a partner is not just having someone to pay your bills, buy your dinner, buy your clothes. Listen to his needs and his dreams.

However, don't go overboard in the gift giving in early months. Hold back on the Porsche and cruises until he shows you some commitment and enthusiasm, without being cajoled. It's a sharing experience we aim to achieve. Remember that money doesn't buy love, so do not buy men clothes and put them through school unless you gave birth to them—they'll step out in all your finery into the arms of another woman. See some of the gifts to give based on my survey (question 30 on page 127). Men like flowers and gifts that represent some thought on your part.

One of my roommates went to the Ivory Coast, spent a weekend in Paris, and made a trip to Los Angeles on three different expense-paid dates within a nine-month period, with three different women. The only thing he did was turn up at the airport and take time off from work. He is now married, but not to any to these three women. He married a woman who would wait no longer than fifteen minutes for him to show up for a dinner date. (He was always late.) So no matter how much you give, it won't help you keep a man if he is not truly interested in you or in love with you.

10. *It's time for an attitude adjustment: Put away that whip!* Many women refer to men as animals that have to be trained. No! No! No! We train pets and dogs, horses, and monkeys; we *respect* our men. We may encourage and suggest certain things that we may want of them, but don't fool yourself into thinking that you have trained them.

During my early days of motherhood, and while running my practice, two women came to my home for consultations. My husband had been commuting between Washington, D.C., and London. He arrived two hours before their consultation. They came early and found him busy with the vacuum cleaner in the study. They both commented to me, "You have him well trained, I see." I resented the comment. "No," I said, "I didn't train him," trying not to show my annoyance. "He came to me ready. He is a kind, considerate man who helps me." He knew I had visitors coming and wanted to do something to help me get ready for my consultation. The man you want should come to you full, ready, and complete. Would you buy a car that had only two gears or a washing machine that had no rinse cycle? Two half people do not make a whole person, only a whole lot of heartache and woe.

11. *Have you settled for Mr. Right Now?* If you are spending time with Mr. Right Now, just for something to do for the heck of it, then when Mr. Right comes along you are not available or ready. Why settle for anything less than the best?

The time you are spending with Mr. Right Now could be given to improving yourself—going to the gym, going to school—rather than being bored or irritated with Mr. Right Now or Mr. Almost Right. If you feel the man is lacking in certain areas, don't settle for something less than the best.

You owe it to yourself. Do not lower your standards to accommodate other people's needs. Do not get caught up in what your mother wants or what your girlfriends think about you. There is always pressure after you get to a certain age and you are not married. I have many friends around the world, each culturally different but all fighting the same old-fashioned view about being single. One of my dearest friends was once criticized by being told that her standards were too high. Of course a woman should set high standards for herself. My girlfriend is six foot one, intelligent, and gorgeous inside and out, so why should she accept anything less than the best? However, be realistic. Don't worry that time is running out and put pressure on yourself and your man. Treat yourself with the utmost respect at all times. If you think you are using him for the moment, think again. It comes right back at you anyway. Whatever you project, that is what you will get. Show the man respect, kindness, and honesty; he will show you the same. If he does not, do not stay around for more. When in doubt, leave him out!

Any time you feel a tinge of doubt about someone, it is your intuitive voice sending you all the signals, warning you that you could be in danger. Listen more to your subconscious voice, because that is what doubt is.

12. *The way to a man's heart is still through his stomach, I'm afraid.* Even if you hate cooking, and strongly believe you are a millennial woman and too busy to be tied to the stove, food is a

very seductive way to entice someone to you. Just learn two or three simple dishes and perfect them. Make them your "specials." Choose what you like and that's easy to cook. I started out with spaghetti. It takes less than six minutes. Add some spices and a sauce and voilà. There are more than thirty different pasta types and a variety of sauces on any supermarket shelf. Later, if you begin to enjoy the reaction to your simple meals, you can progress to lobster thermidor or duck à l'orange. (I married a carnivorous man who became a vegetarian, so now it is tofu baked, grilled, and sautéed.) I'm not saying you should become a kitchen slave with an apron around your waist seven nights a week. Just pull out your skills a few times so the man knows you can cook. You don't become his mother or his short-order chef.

Good Food Guide

· Salads come prepacked and ready to serve. Just remember to provide some color (e.g., tomatoes, red and yellow bell peppers, red cabbage). And make sure to use the best dressing— that's what makes them undress for you!

· Seafood is also easy to cook and often comes precooked. (Do you remember Bubba in *Forrest Gump,* and how many different ways he could prepare shrimp?) Warning: Don't leave seafood unrefrigerated for long. You will both end up with an upset stomach and that will not be romantic at all. The man may never eat from your kitchen again.

· Boil-in-the-bag rices take five minutes, max.

· Soup and salads are great with garlic bread. You can use canned soup as long as you toss some fresh herbs on top to make it look homemade.

· Become a spice girl. Experiment with different herbs and

spices that rapidly change the taste of the same foods. Acquaint yourself with garlic, ginger, coriander, cilantro, and rosemary.

Cooking does not have to be a regular thing, but the man should know that you can do it and do it well. Save your skills for special times. We are busy women with reports to write and other commitments. (If you wish to be a slave, try a room other than the kitchen.)

A dear friend of mine didn't know how to cook and had no desire to learn either. She was a millennial woman who felt that cooking was a subservient act, a thing of the past, a role important in her mother's life. It wasn't until after she split with her husband that she realized the importance of cooking for her mate. Her first husband never told her how much he hated the fact that she had no interest in cooking until their marriage was over. (If you do not believe me, see what the survey says: Question 34 on page 127.)

Food Foreplay

Toppings

| Ice Cream | Whipped Cream | Honey |
| Chocolate | Caramel | |

Fruits

| Strawberries | Black Cherries | Grapes |
| Lychees | Mangoes | Peaches |

Beverages

Champagne, of course, with orange juice or strawberries.
Cocktails: piña coladas, screwballs, margaritas, Up Against the Walls, and Harvey Wallbangers are all interesting combinations of alcohol and fruit.

13. Are you getting tuned up by a maintenance man? If you are be-tween relationships and you are being maintained, be discreet; do not discuss it with your girlfriends. You may find your provider is servicing a wider area than you think. Remember, safe sex at all times. Any relationship you are in, either long-term or one-night stands, you are actually sleeping with at least twenty other people unless you are sleeping with a vir-gin. In Jamaica there is a new condom called Slam, so tell him if he wants to bam he has to put on a Slam.

A friend of mine told me that while she was in between re-lationships, she planned to go out and have some fun, the way men do. "Don't forget to take care of yourself," I suggested, sounding like her mother. "I'm on the pill," she said confi-dently. "No, no," I replied. "Not from getting pregnant but from getting hepatitis B, gonorrhea, chlamydia, herpes, syphilis, or HIV/AIDS." You're not likely to die from having a baby, but you could easily die from not protecting yourself. There are still many women not protecting themselves. The Pill and the diaphragm are not sufficient protection anymore. Don't wait for the man to bring home the protection—pro-vide your own. Keep your health and your life in your hands, and keep this statistic in your head: As of 1998, a total of 115,907 women in the United States had been diagnosed with AIDS. African-American women comprised the largest number, 65,646; white women numbered 25,636; Latin American women numbered 23,326; Asian women num-bered 591; and Native American women numbered 332.

Be discreet about past relationships. Men really don't want to know. No matter how much they may say they are open, liberal, and want you to be honest, they really don't. Whether it is five men, fifteen, or fifty, keep it to yourself. As one man bluntly put it, "I liked that lady but she had too many miles on her clock. How much of a lady can she be?"

14. *How soon do you mention the* M *word?* Leave the *M* word out of the conversation for the moment, or as long as you are able. Which *M* word? Money—no. Masturbation—no. *Marriage.* Even if he is the one, wait a little while. You can propose if you are a millennial woman, but don't pressure for a commitment, and don't propose unless you are really ready for the answer. And don't propose a second time. Actions speak louder than words. You will know when the time is right and you are both ready. If he keeps suggesting that you are both "just friends," that is your first clue: he's trying to keep you at bay. If you are still dating after five years, don't expect a ring or wedding bells unless you are both in college.

15. *Sisterhood is powerful; make women your friends.* Trust your sisters more. Love them more, respect them more. They are a reflection of you. Do not compete with them. Your time will come. Do not flirt with their men. My survey says 85 percent of men have slept with their woman's girlfriend, best friend, or sister. Though this is hard to believe, I was encouraged to include this question in my survey by a man, so obviously this fact is known among men. Do not be flattered by their advances; be true to your girlfriends and yourself. Tell the man he should get stepping and tell the friend why you told him to do so. If you are united with each other, less cheating will occur. When I was single, I always asked all my girlfriends whether the man I was seeing had anyone else out there. My sources were usually quite reliable. A few boyfriends got busted very early in their game. Once my cousin and her girlfriend found out that they were dating the same man. He arranged

to take my cousin to the movies on Friday and her girlfriend on Saturday. The girlfriend decided she would arrive on Friday with my cousin. They arrived arm in arm. I wish I had been there to see his face. The perfect Kodak moment!

Can someone help me here? I have two questions for the ladies. Can you tell me why it is that we will buy expensive tickets to see Aretha or Patti and take a man, but would not do the same for a girlfriend, a cousin, or a sister? Why is it that we desert our friends and family when someone new comes into our lives?

Yes, you know who you are! Everyone knows when you have a man in your life, because no one ever sees you; you don't stay in touch. We understand, but don't throw us out. We have to help plan the wedding when it comes. Or let you cry on our shoulders when the relationship doesn't work out. So keep in touch. Please do not give up your girlfriends for your man. Include him, include us. He enhances your destiny, he does not determine it.

A word about cheating with married men. Say no to drugs and married men every time. When married men approach you, charming, charismatic, with compliments, saying, "My wife does not understand me," "I am only there for the children," "We do not make love anymore," remember, *don't* fall for them. Ten years later he'll still be leaving his wife, or waiting for the baby to finish her master's degree. Just say no and save yourself heartbreak. You cannot and should not disrespect yourself. You are made in the same image as the woman the man is married to. To be intimate with him means disrespecting yourself and his wife. When he is free you want to be number three: the first two dates after his breakup will have to deal with comparisons and complaints, and you don't need those either. Getting through a divorce is painful and heart-wrenching at times. Would you rather be the shoulder he'll cry on or the shoulder he will rest his head on in days and nights to come?

Married-Men Alert

- The most obvious way to identify a married man is the fact that you cannot call him at home. You have every other number except that one.
- You cannot see him on weekends and holidays, except for fleeting moments. You will always get your Christmas gift the day after Christmas. You know the routine if you have been there.
- You know the man is married when he cannot be seen with you in public too often, or he can't be affectionate with you in public.
- If you invite him to social events, he constantly gives excuses as to why he can't be there.
- He's sleeping with you, but he tells you, "We are just friends."

The Players Alert

Players are very similar to married men, with a few extras.

There is the "Me Soon Come" man. In the Caribbean they say, "Me soon come." These soon-come men have spread themselves all over the globe. They are coming back but they give you no specific time. When I was in college, I dated a soon-come man. He would say, "Me soon come," and I thought he meant what he said. He turned up unannounced three months later, with no real explanation. I had already assumed that everything was off between us. If the man takes you to a party and says that, and then comes back four or five dances later, there is someone else in the room he also has to keep happy.

Then there are the Vampires or the Night Doctors. They are the ones you never see in the daytime. They come out only at night, to visit you at 2 A.M., to sleep in your bed.

The Video Man brings a video and a meal to your home under the guise that he wants a romantic evening alone. You do not ever meet his friends. In fact, you never meet anybody. When the man tells you he is private and wants to keep the relationship private, he's basically telling you not to talk about him to your girlfriends. He might be sleeping with one of them too. This man can't give out a phone number. He gives you a pager number or a cell phone number, or you can only call him at the office as Miss X.

Watch out for special events. Don't be fooled by roses sent on Valentine's Day, when the man tells you he'll be out of town. This past Valentine's Day I ran my own investigation. I called four of my male (player) friends and, guess what? They were all at home. They shared with me that they had sent roses and gifts to all their prospective mates but did not want to spend the evening with any of them because it was sending the wrong message—that they may be more serious than they were. Flowers can mean nothing without the person there with you. They may be a camouflage for other feelings, such as guilt, or they may represent no more than tradition or politeness. Unfortunately, they don't always mean love. Don't get caught up in the hype.

16. Make a playboy, Casanova, gigolo, or player your best friend. Yours will be one less heart he can break, and you can learn a lot from his tricks. Everything I ever wanted to know about men, I learned from them, including my father. Girlfriends, sisters, and mothers can tell you only so much. I once dated a young man, and one of my male friends warned me about him: "Beware of that dog."

"Oh," I said, quite innocently. "He's really very nice."

"Trust me, Bev," my friend warned. "I know a dog when I see one. Remember, I *am* one." My friend saved me from a heartbreak situation.

17. *Don't put men in a kennel; they are not dogs.* I cannot stand to hear women refer to men as "dogs," mainly because I was raised by a quiet, genteel, diligent Jamaican man. I married a hardworking African-American man, and I'm now raising a beautiful, international, renaissance man. If you are a mother raising a son, consider the negative messages you are sending to his young, impressionable mind by the use of such a word. Never mind what you have experienced with other men, think of the "new" man you are raising. *Think* how you can create change so that your son, a nephew, or a younger brother can benefit from your experiences. When you treat men with disrespect, you are disrespecting the young boys and males in your own life. How can they become worthy?

Be responsible for your own actions, not the man's. I hear women say that men lie, men cheat, men disrespect them. They did all this without your help? Men can do to you only what you allow them to do. Men tell you what you want to hear in one evening. Command respect and you will receive it. Be respectful to yourself and your man.

I overheard my roommate having three consecutive conversations with three different women. Whatever their needs were, he accommodated them verbally with false promises.

He said whatever they wanted to hear. He would click over to the next conversation and start all over again. I was so disgusted with him by the third call, I left the room. I'm not sure how many more lies he told that night.

Find out first what a man's needs are before you express yours. Do they fit together? If not, keep stepping. You will trust men more when you learn to trust yourself first. You set yourself up for failure every time if you don't trust your own judgment. Stop, and listen to your intuition, not your heart. Don't wait for the man's approval, his acceptance, his calls. Set your own path and pave your own way. Maybe he will follow if you excite him enough.

18. Be his friend when you meet him, not his mother. It takes the pressure off dating. When a man feels safe around you, he will relax, bring his guard down, and tell you everything. Consider him the way you would a girlfriend. If your girlfriend did not call you for a few days, would you be mad at her? Share information with him. Tell him what you like, what you feel. He cannot read your mind. If you marry him, you will be his partner, his best friend, his soul mate—whatever you want to call him. So treat him like you would a sister, friend, or a close girlfriend. Men have been hurt too. The more relaxed the man is around you, the more he will want to share his ideas, his music, and his interests with you, just as you would with your girlfriends. The only difference will be the level of intimacy between you and the man, if you choose to take your relationship to another level. So stop all the guessing games.

19. Are you competing with his children? If the man has children, love them and accept them. They are a part of his life and always will be, so don't try to compete with them. You would want him to do the same with your children, wouldn't you? However, if you have children, don't introduce them too early in the relationship. Protect your children until you are really sure of whom you are bringing home for dinner.

Don't send your children mixed messages. They already have a father, even if he's not around, so don't confuse them with a dad of the month. This is especially the case if you have girls. Think of the message you are sending your kids if they see you with several different partners.

Do not be angry if you have to wait while he does Daddy things with his little girl. There is nothing sexier to me than a man who takes care of his children, regardless of his relationship with the children's mother.

20. *Don't take your partner for granted.* Say what you mean, and mean what you say.

I had a friend who used to treat her husband badly. She disrespected him in front of his friends and ridiculed him. He stayed in the marriage for twelve years because of his children. She caused him to lose his self-esteem because he didn't want to break up his family. One day he decided he'd had enough and left, leaving her with the three girls. She cried and was depressed for almost a year. I was surprised, because this was the first time I had heard or seen her show any feeling for him.

Another friend told me his wife showed him very little interest or affection, often turning her back on his nightly advances. He made many suggestions to her, including that they both seek counseling to help resolve their differences. She felt there was no need because there was nothing wrong within their marriage. He tried to persuade her in different ways but nothing worked. He stayed in his loveless marriage for more than nine years and spent most of his social time in bars. One day he left. Within weeks he was dating someone who had had her eye on him for a long time. He is now with a woman who appreciates him for who he is and is very happy in his new relationship. His wife was shocked that he left so suddenly, moving out of their newly purchased home. She said she did not realize that anything was wrong and that he was so unhappy. She begged him to come back, but it was too late. Do not take your partner for granted. Whatever it took to capture him, you still have to continue to keep the passion flowing. Stay beautiful. Enhance your powers intellectually, physically, and sexually. Honor a good man. He's hard to find. There are many single women waiting to replace you.

Remember, you seduce a man with the three *E*'s: Be *evasive, enhance* your powers, and get the man *excited* (be smart, be unique, be happy).

Love Connection: Eight Hot Spots to Meet Men

1. Through friends or family members. This represents a safe referral or a point of reference, a useful jump start. It is a rule that every married woman who has a single friend should discreetly look for a partner for her. If she places three couples together, then she is secured a space in heaven. So guess where I am going! "Married women are less threatening," a man once told me at a dinner party. It is easier to talk to them, he pointed out, because they don't want anything from you; the exchange is much easier because they don't have to keep a guard up. As a married woman, you can learn everything you want to know about a man and pass on the information to a single friend. Everyone that I have matched is still married.

2. *Intimate social events, e.g., dinner parties and weddings.* In my college days I had two very close friends I used to spend a lot of time with. We threw many dinner parties that helped us to get to know our prospective partners. You can find out a lot about someone over a plate of food. A dinner setting stimulates conversation. You can learn what a man knows of etiquette and other table topics. Does he say grace, is he familiar with an à la carte menu, the wineglasses, the silverware? Is he punctual? What are his favorite topics of conversation beyond sports?

Weddings are always a good place to meet someone. You can guarantee that if a man is single at a wedding, he is *single*. Most men hate attending events like this and usually bring along someone even if the relationship is only halfway serious, just to break the boredom of the day.

3. *At work.* We spend so much time on our jobs working with people it is easy to become attracted to a fellow worker. However, it can be a little awkward, and calls for maximum discretion. Tread carefully here, because things could blow up in your face, especially if he is flirting with other coworkers. When a man approaches you at work, pay attention to those he is *not* talking to; he may have been flirting with one (or more) of them. Be very careful not to get caught up in any sexual-harassment charges by scorned admirers; at the same time, don't use it against a man if he shuns you. An office romance can be either a great hit or a terrible embarrassment if it does not work out. My attitude in this area has changed over the past fifteen years, as so many people I have met have found

their partner in the workplace. When I was a manager in the UK, I could always tell who was zooming in on whom. The parties involved never spoke to each other or gave each other direct eye contact in the office. I once managed a software house that employed sixty men. I had a secretary who looked like Debbie Harry. Of course the men were falling all over her. She dated one of the consultants, although I advised her not to. Fortunately, she did not listen to me. Now she is happily married, with two sons, and living in Canada.

4. Colleges, conventions, and conferences. Here you can meet like-minded people: birds of a feather flock together. In the average course of the year, your given profession has a series of conferences or seminars throughout the country and worldwide. These events have endless social activities and are educational and inspiring. Start finding out where these conferences are held and make a promise to be there the next time. They are a prime opportunity to travel, surround yourself with other professionals, educate and motivate yourself, and socialize with interesting professional people. The one drawback may be that you may not want to date someone in your field. A friend of mine, a dentist, found a way around this. She met her husband, an engineer, at a writers' conference.

There are various conventions held in different cities; look up your local convention center and see what events are coming to town. When the Million Man March was held here in D.C., many of my girlfriends were calling me, asking if they could come and stay with me for the weekend. Apart from professional conferences, there are fraternal organizations—recently I heard that more than three thousand fraternity brothers met in New Orleans—and don't forget religious events and cruises also.

5. *Supermarkets.* See what is in the man's cart. A cart heavily laden with groceries is not the sign of a single man. If you find no baby food, no female toiletries, that's a good start. Canned food or prepacked food and single dinners are what you are looking for.

6. *In transit—especially in airports and on trains, buses, and planes.* Look at the passengers, not the service providers. The service providers are there to serve the public and that is exactly what they do. You'll probably like what they say to you, but they say the same thing to everyone, so don't be flattered and get caught up in their game. And remember, you never see unemployed people hanging out at airports.

7. *At the gym.* Look for the regulars and the ones that look like they are serious about being there. Their bodies should provide you clues. You may have to be the one to initiate a conversation, because they are too busy pumping iron. Ignore the ones that approach you and are attending occasionally and have nothing to show but fancy gym clothes. If you are intimidated by the crowds, try early morning, when they are not so crowded. Learn to swim. When I go to the pool I rarely see women in the water. Don't worry about your hair; just use a good conditioner. That's usually what stops a lot of women from enjoying the pool and the endless men who love the water.

8. *Roommates.* Need to share expenses, or just want companionship? Find a roommate. (That's how I met my man.)

You start off as friends and you get to know the man's interests and habits and his way of treating other women. My

smooth-talking man had several pusuers; my phone was ring-
ing off the hook. However, he always had respect for those
who called for him.

Forget the Hype: Where Not to Meet Men

1. Clubs and bars. These are not good places to meet someone. You have no point of reference with regard to the
strangers who gather there. The place can become a meat
market. If you do happen to meet someone and cannot resist
him, don't give him your number—instead, take his—and do
not let him take you home. Get to know the man first by
phone and meet him in a public place, e.g., for lunch. A lunch
date is a good way to begin. Always let someone know where
you are going and whom you will be with.

2. Parties. Like bars, parties are places where people meet in a
cloud of smoke and booze. They too can be a meat market.
Unless the hostess can tell you about the man you are interested in, the same rules apply as above. Be careful what you
drink and watch how your drink is being prepared. Preferably
get a drink from a can or bottle that has not been opened, so
no one has a chance to slip anything in it. There have been in-
cidents where women have been subjected to sexual activity
without their knowledge because they have been drugged, so
be careful and mindful. Also, do not drink too much when you
are out on your dates. Keep your mind clear and listen to and
observe everything that is going on around you.

3. Church. The purpose of the church is not to provide members of the congregation with prospective partners. A lot of

single men admitted to me that this is the place they can guarantee they can score. Many of them do not go to pray, they go
to prey.

Most congregations are 70 percent or more female. Many
single women are looking for spiritual guidance. Some are
vulnerable, some are lonely. If you happen to spot a handsome
honey in the pews, be careful; he could be a wolf in sheep's
clothing. Don't become his prey. Be sure to check him out
from a reliable source in the church. That may not always be
the minister either. Usually men seeking to score jump from
church to church, leaving many broken hearts behind. I apol-
ogize to the genuinely religious men that go to church to
worship, who may suffer by association with the others. Also
be careful of the ministers who have wives and several mis-
tresses and mismanage funds! Respect your minister but remember he is a man with feelings also.

4. *The beach.* Can you get your groove back on vacation?
Highly unlikely. Even though it worked for Terry McMillan
(author of *How Stella Got her Groove Back*) and her husband,
Jonathan Plummer, they are two unique individuals who were
lucky enough to be able to step out and claim their love. Unfortunately, many of the island dates are hustling on the
beaches to get visas to leave their native islands. Their swift,
sexy, sweet jive talk is part of the island package. Enjoy them,
but if you don't want to get burned, beware of these bronzed,
buffed beauties.

5. *The Internet.* Definitely not! This is too dangerous. The
movie *You've Got Mail* may seem encouraging, but remember,
you are still communicating with a stranger whose background is unknown to you and largely uncheckable—and you

don't even have the benefit of the vibes you get when you're in a man's presence. Do not get lured into his web; you may be on the right page for only a brief moment. Anyone can be smooth on a keyboard.

So You Get a Date—Now What?

Lunch together is good for a first date. Use your lunch break for this purpose. A lunch date is quick, easy, and inexpensive. If this date goes great, you can make plans to see the man again. Offer to pay your half, and do not choose the most expensive item on the menu if he is paying. Not only is it bad manners, he will want to be rewarded in kind for his dollars spent.

On future dates, don't forget the four C's in case of an emergency.

1. A cell phone. Every woman should own a cell phone; you'll need to call for help if you have a breakdown—or if he decides not to be a gentleman and take you home.
2. A credit card (just in case he forgets his).
3. Cash, in case you have to leave him in a hurry and you need to catch a cab. Do not spend time with someone if he is making you feel uncomfortable or uneasy or you just don't feel good around him. Cash should always be your getaway plan or your "vex" money, as my father used to call it.
4. Condoms, just in case you really can't resist his charm. If you love your life, do not put your life in somebody else's hands. Be sure to use a condom. You may regret sleeping with him later, but no need to regret it nine months later, or when you test positive for HIV/AIDS.

Always let someone know where you are going and who you are with. Sometimes we end up on the dating circuit so long that we don't want to talk about our prospective dates until we've had a chance to check them out. But tell just one person in case he turns out to be a knucklehead.

Ms. Vulnerable, stay home with a good movie or a book. Don't go out on dates when you are on the rebound. No need to be out there with your guard completely down. You will regret it later. You cannot make clear decisions when you are vulnerable. Decisions then are usually made for the wrong reasons. If you are on the rebound, you want to get revenge, to nurse your ego. Wait until you are in a better frame of mind.

Keep an open mind. Do not set limits to race, gender, age, or status. There are more potential partners out there than you think.

CREATE YOUR OWN PATH

Life is a journey. Plan your life to be as exciting and as great as you want it to be. Look at all aspects of your life. Is it how it should be? If you owned your own business, you would have to create a business plan. Well, why not create your own road map and ask yourself where you want to be five years from now? Do you know?

Write out plans for all the areas of your life. At any given time your life could change. You take a different path, you make a wrong decision. Fate controls where we are going to be. Tomorrow is not guaranteed to you, so do something positive and profound each and every day. The present is indeed "a present," a gift from the Creator that is sent today.

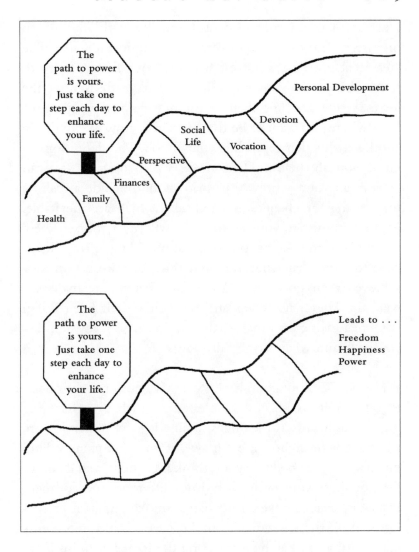

In the above illustration, a path has been designed to assist you with your planning. Look at each aspect of your life, and insert your level of contentment. How can you improve it? Give yourself a score from zero to ten, ten being the highest score and level of contentment. Be honest with yourself; no one has to see these scores. Write a score in each area. The areas that scored the lowest become your first priority to make changes in your life. On the blank path, transfer the lowest scores first, and then on the outside of the path, consider where you want to be five years from now. Write this in another color that represents your mood. The definitions to guide you are below. Then create a plan of how you can achieve all your desires. Your plan should include a realistic time frame for changes and setbacks, which are inevitable. Make a promise to yourself that you will meet yourself there five years from now, or sooner. Trust me. Many of my clients have told me that when they put this plan into action they achieved their goals and dreams long before the five years were up. They have to update and review their path. When you create your road map, make it a journey of joy and discovery. Claim what is rightfully yours.

1. Health. Without good health you have nothing. Your body is your temple. Respect it. Be blessed with what you have: big hips, small breasts, thick thighs, skinny legs. Whether you are a size eight or eighteen, be in awe of your uniqueness. Find one part of your body that you think is beautiful and flaunt it. Do not abuse your body with drugs, fast food, and fast men. If you are a nonsmoker, don't date a smoker. Apart from suffering from the secondhand smoke, every time you are intimate with a smoker, he is injecting the toxins from his body into yours. By no means allow anyone to abuse you physically or mentally.

Have you had all your regular health checks? Pap smears, mammograms, HIV tests?

When you prepare yourself for your monthly breast self-examination, remember that your breasts usually do not hurt when cancer begins to grow there; that is why it goes undetected for a long time. Be sure your body is in perfect condition, or as good as you can get it. If you are diligent, many diseases can be cured in the early stages before they spread too far.

2. *Family.* How do you define your family? Your parents and siblings, your partner and children?

How do you feel about the people who are close to you in your life? Is there any family member that you would like to make peace with? Someone you are still angry with? The only person who is suffering from this situation is you. The other person is getting on with his or her life regardless of how you feel. Address the problem. Make a change to forgive and forget and let it go. Let those you love know. Show your appreciation in every way you can. You will never know when a person is going to be taken from you forever. Light a candle for those you have lost and miss. Are you wasting time in a stagnant relationship when you could be spending time with those who love you unconditionally? Know them, seek them out, and cherish the time you have with them.

3. *Finances.* Do you have all your finances in order? I'm not talking just about credit cards debts. Do you have a will? If you have children, have you made plans for their care if something happens to you suddenly? If you are a single mother, you should give clear instructions as to who will take care of your children when you are gone. They are precious to you; they should not be left without proper instructions for their care. Your loss would be traumatic, so make the transition for them as smooth as possible. With God's love you will be around to

play with your grandchildren. Many women tell me that they don't have anything to bequeath and do not need a will, but as long as you are working, you have assets. There may be life insurance, at least. You are usually worth more dead than alive. Who will get this if you die and you have no children?

4. Perspective. How do you feel about social issues? Are you informed in all such areas as much as you should be? How could you become more aware of them, more actively involved in your community? Look into your local community activities and see what part you can play. Like they say, reach out and touch someone. The more you give, the more you receive.

5. Social life. Are you doing all the things you want to do socially? Going to the theater? Are you traveling, eating out, visiting friends? Whatever it is that is lacking, look at ways to enhance this area of your life, even if it is only once a month. As working individuals with many responsibilities, we sometimes find it hard to make time to just hang out and have some fun. Laugh a little, kick off your shoes, and dance on the beach. Make a list of things you can do to put more fun in your life and to engage in social activity, which could relieve your stress and improve your state of mind.

Promise yourself to do this, and keep the promise. Usually when you take yourself out of a bad situation, it really isn't so bad when you come back to it. Sometimes you need to take your head out of the sand and come up for air.

Laughter can be a great healer. Share your hopes and desires with those you trust. Let them all hang out. If they are locked inside, there is no room for growth. The spirit needs to hear it. You call it out and summon it to you.

6. *Vocation.* You may hate your job, but while you are there, learn as much as you can. Every skill is transferrable, so do the best you can. You may find the position you have is not so bad once you start looking at it as more than just a salary. Make it your financial safety net until you can make your transition. If you want to have your own business, look at what you can learn in someone else's business before you depart to set up your own. Go back to school; use your lunchtime to research new opportunities or to study. Stop making excuses. Follow your instincts. Too many waking hours are spent on the job if you hate it. Make plans to move from the job you loathe to a position you love. Realistically, a career transition can take two to three years, so pace yourself.

7. *Devotion.* Perhaps you don't like going to church. Devotion is about centering yourself, devoting time to listen to your inner voice, time to receive and give thanks for your blessings. Ask yourself what your soul's purpose is here on this earth and whether you are living it. Devotion comes in many forms. It could be meditating, praying, chanting. You should have an understanding of or a connection to your higher spiritual being and how everything is made possible for you through a higher force. Don't become pious and self-righteous just because you find yourself in church every Sunday. You still need to reach out into the community and touch someone else's life.

8. *Personal development.* Are you working to make yourself the very best you can be in all the above areas? This type of work is vital because you are a work of art in progress. Make the most of yourself by attending the various forums that are avail-

able to you. You may add new light, meaning to your life. If dating has been a nightmare in the past, and you are afraid to step out for fear of being hurt, look at yourself in the mirror. What can you change about yourself? What are the lessons you have learned from your past experiences? How can you do things differently next time? Everything we experience happens for a reason. There are no coincidences. A door closes but there is always a window open for another opportunity to enhance your life. Next time you date, love like you have never been hurt before, and live as if there is no tomorrow.

Now that you have considered all these aspects, all the above should be in order before you begin to include another person in your life. When he joins you, he should enhance what you have and not determine who you are. Life is a journey. Embrace each day and live it to the fullest. Do not worry about what you do not have. Feel blessed with what you have and enjoy the moment. It does not mean you cannot plan and strive for a better future. Continue each day of your amazing journey, thankful and at peace with yourself. Whatever you want in life you *can* achieve.

One of the quickest ways to find your soul mate is first to stop looking for him. Find yourself and *your* soul first. Be clear about what you want and love about yourself. Be in awe of your own uniqueness. It is hard to love another if you cannot begin with yourself. When your mind and soul are clear, you can trust your judgment readily and easily. Everything else will fall into place.

SELF-TEST

Ask yourself all the following questions and answer them honestly. Start with, Am I the kind of person I would like to marry? Whatever you are looking for in your mate, be sure you already have in yourself. Whatever material acquisitions you want from a man, you should get them for yourself.

1. *Who am I? How do I see myself?* Describe yourself with powerful words.

2. *What are my needs?*

3. *What are my attributes?*

4. *What are my weaknesses?*

5. *How can I make changes to overcome some of my weaknesses?*

6. *What kind of man do I want?* Write your own shopping list of characteristics you want in your partner.

7. *What can I live without?* Write a list of what you definitely don't want in your partner. Expand on the list from the three requested at the beginning of the book (see page 13). Once you have made your list, make a commitment to yourself not to settle for anyone with those negatives.

8. *What do I have to offer?* List what you will bring to the relationship. Often in our search we are looking for what we can get from our partners, rather than what we can offer to enhance the relationship.

9. *What are my reasons for wanting to be married?* Love, companionship, security, status, money? Be honest. No one has to see these answers but you.

10. *Do I know my own body?* In order to get what you want, you have to know what you like. Make a list of all the things you like sexually.

11. *What is my ultimate sexual fantasy?*

12. *Do I know how to ask for what I want without making my partner feel inadequate?*

13. *Which is more important—size or skill?* Some of the men I interviewed wanted to know this. Look at your *y*'s and *g*'s to determine your own energy level and sex drive.

14. *If Mr. Write showed up tomorrow, what would be his purpose in my life?*

Prepare your own self-analysis from your handwriting. Write a few sentences.

· How do you cross your *t*'s (motivation)?
· How do you see yourself? What is your self-image?
· How do you communicate?
· What is your sex drive?
· How do you respond emotionally? (Look at the slant.)
· Are you stubborn?
· How do you process information?

   Your journey began a long time ago. You may have taken a few wrong paths. Start your journey without a man; do not postpone living, waiting for him to come. He will catch up with you when you are ready and the time is right. Step out and take a leap of faith and claim what is rightfully yours.

Do you believe in the miracle of love? I still do!

Stay beautiful! Stay powerful! Stay in touch with the power of your uniqueness.

MIRROR, MIRROR ON THE WALL

Look in the mirror, what do you see?
Are you the woman you want to be?
Positive, powerful, and passionate.
Stepping proudly in your glory.
Be mad, be sad, be bad,
be mean to keep them keen.
Whatever you do
will come back to you,
so be happy or be blessed.
Whatever you project is what you will get.
Be sweet and turn up the heat,
they will swarm you, like bees to honey.
So honey, be unique, be true to you.
Look in the mirror, what do you see?
Are you the woman you want to be?

—Beverley East

Quick Find

A

𝒜 𝑎 Acquisitive

𝒜 𝔞 Attention seeking

𝑎 Candid/frank

𝒜𝒜𝑎 Cautious

𝑎 Compulsive liar

𝜎 𝑎 Deceitful

𝑎 Drug abuser

𝑎 Evasive

𝑎 Nurturing

𝑎 Resentful

𝑎 Secretive

𝑎 Self-deceitful

𝒂 Sensual

𝑎 Silent/closed communicator

𝑢 Talkative

B

𝓑 𝑏 Direct

𝑏 Good business sense

𝓑 𝑏 Humorous

𝑏 𝑏 Inhibited/reserved

𝓑 𝑏 Jealous

𝑏 Leisurely

𝑏 Positive

𝑏 Sensual

𝑏 Spiritual/philosophical

ᖯ Temper
Bb Uninhibited

C

ᴄ Acquisitive
C_ Cautious
ℰ Compulsive liar
C Direct
ᴄ Drug abuser
ℓ Resentful
C Temper
C Uninhibited

D

d Arrogant
ᴅ Attention seeking
ᴅ Book lover
d Cautious
d d Compulsive liar
d Conceited
d ᴅ Deceitful
d Dignified
D d Direct
dʟ Drug abuser
dʟ Empathetic

d Evasive
d Fatalistic
d Frank/direct
d Independent
⏐ ᴅ Inhibited
d Matter-of-fact
d Positive
dˣ Proud
d Relentless
d Resentful
ᴅ Reserved/shy
dd Self-conscious
d Sensitive to criticism
d Supersensitive
d Stubborn
d Sensual
d Self-deceitful
d Talkative
d Uninhibited
dˣ Vain

E

ℓ ℓ Acquisitive
ℓ Attention seeking

ℰ Book lover
℮ Broad-minded
ℯ Cautious
ℰ Cultured
E Direct
ℛ Drug abuser
ℯ Generous
ℯ Good listener
ℯ Fatalistic
⊂ Inhibited
⟍ Matter-of-fact
ℓ ℮ Narrow-minded
ℯ Resentful
e Sensual
ℯ Tolerant
Eℯ Uninhibited

F

ƒ Acquisitive
F ƒ Direct
ƒ ƒ Disorganized
F Factual
ƒ Fluid
ƒ Idea man
Hƒ Inhibited

ƒ Organized, balanced
ƒ Organizes through action
ƒ Persistent
ⱷ ⱷ Positive
δ ƒ Rejection
ƒ Restless
F Simplicity
ƒ↗ ƒ Uncompromising
⊢ Uninhibited

G

9 Aggressive
9 A bluffer
9 Clannish
ℊ Cultured
ɣ ℊ Denial of sexual pleasures
ℊ Determined
G ℊ Direct
ℊ Drug abuser
ℊ Extravagant
ℊ Fatalistic

𝟪 𝑔 Fluid

℞ 𝑔 𝑔 Frustrated lover

𝑔 Irresponsible

𝑞 Loner

𝑔 Lover man

𝑔 The Night Nurse

𝑔 No stamina/
determination

𝑔 Only interested in
the chase

𝑞 𝑔 Restless

𝑞 Selective

𝐠 Sensual

𝑔 Sexual aggression

𝑔 Sexual agility

𝑔 Sexual tyrant

𝑔 Social

𝑔 The Stroker

𝑞 Suppressed sexual
desire

𝑞𝑔𝑞 Unsettled libido

H

𝒽 Acquisitive

𝗁 Analytical

H 𝗁 Direct

𝗁 Drug abuser

𝒽 Hesitant

𝗁 Humorous

𝗁 Initiative

𝗁 Interested in
spiritual and
philosophical
concepts

H 𝗁 Jealous

𝒽 Keen/quick-
minded

𝗁 Positive

𝒽 Possible learning
disability

𝒽 Practical
imagination

𝒽 Repressed

𝒽 Resentful

h 𝒽 Sensual

𝒳 Shy/reserved

H𝗁 Simple

𝒽 Spiritual

Ⳑ Superficial

𝗁 Temper

H𝗁 Uninhibited

𝒽 Worried

I

- ℒ Acquisitive
- ℐ Adaptable
- ℒ Aggressive
- ℒ Cautious
- ⅃ Conforming
- ℒ Contrary
- ℒ Courageous
- ℨ Demanding
- /am /am Depressed
- ℐ Dignified
- ℐℒ Egotistic
- ℒ Emotional
- ─ℐ─ Energetic
- ─ℐ─ Enthusiastic
- ℨℐ─ Extroverted
- ℒ Fearful
- ℒ Feelings of inadequacy
- . . ‖ℓ Idealistic
- ℓℓ Immature
- ⎮ Independent
- ℐ\ Introverted
- ℐ Irresponsible
- ℒam /am Lack of self-confidence

- ℐℙ Loose cannon
- ⅃ Maternal influence
- ℨ /am Modest
- ℊ $ Money hungry
- ⅃ Paternal influence
- ⎮ℐℐ Proud
- ℒ Refined
- ℐ Reserved
- ℐℐ⎮ Self-absorbed
- ⎮ℐ Self-confident
- ✓ ℨ Timid
- ℨ Unsociable

i

- ℓ Acquisitive
- ⎿ Cautious
- ℓ ℓ Critical
- ⎮ ⎮ Direct
- ℓ Drug abuser
- ⎮ ℓ Forgetful
- ℓ ℓ Good attention to detail
- ℓ Hesitant
- ℓ Humorous
- ℓ ℓ Idiosyncratic

ᒷ Impatient

ᒎ Irritable

ᒌ Loyal

ᒎ Procrastinating

ᒌ Self-critical

ᑌ Sensual

ᒌ ᒐ Sincere

J

ᒉ ᒉ Acquisitive

Ɣ Aggressive

ɟ ɟ A bluffer

ᒎ Desire for change

ᒎ ᒍ Direct

ᒎ Idiosyncratic

ᒎ Irritable

ᒍ Jealous

ɟ Loyal/sincere

ᒎ Procrastinating

ᒎ Resentful

ɟ Sensual

K

ᒃ Aloof

ᒃ Cautious

ᒃ Defensive

ᒃ Direct

ᒃ Good ethics/morals

ᒃ Inhibited

ᒃ Jealous

ᒃ Nervous

ᒃ ᒃ Temper

ᒃ Uninhibited

L

ᒪ ᒪ Direct

ᒪ Exaggerated imagination

ᒪ Generous

ᒪᒪ Good ethics/morals

ᒪ Greedy

ᒪ Inhibited

ᒪ Moderate imagination

ᒪ Relentless

ᒪ Restricted imagination

ᒪᒪ Self-conscious

ᒪ Sexual Peacock

ᒪ Showy

/ Spiritual
   imagination

ℓ ∠ Uninhibited

M

M Analytical

m m Cautious

ᴎ ᴎ Desire for attention

ơm Desire for
   responsibility

m̂ Diplomatic

M Direct

ơh Envious

ᴗm Humorous

ᵱm Jealous

ᴎ Methodical mind

ᴗm Possessive

ᴎ Possible learning
   disability

m Repressed

ᴪ Reserved

m̃ Self-conscious

me Self-reliant

M m Sensual

Mₐₙ Sexual Peacock

M Sharp, quick

ᴗᴗ Superficial

ᴗᴗ ᵐ Temper

ᴎ Worried

N

ᴨ Accumulative

ᴧ Acquisitive

ᴎ Analytical

ᴎ ᴧ Cautious

ᴎ ᴧ Desire for
   attention

ᴧ Desire for
   responsibility

ħ Diplomatic

N Direct

ᴗᴨ Humorous

ᴪ Inhibited

ᴨ Repressed

ᴨ̃ Self-conscious

N ᴧ Sensual

ᴎ ᴨ Uninhibited

ᴧ Worried

O

◑	☯	Compulsive liar
♂	⍺	Deceitful
	○	Direct/frank
	☯	Evasive
	℘	Resentful
	⍺	Secretive
	⌀	Self-deceitful
	O	Sensual
	○	Talkative

P

⊬	Aggressive
⊦	Argumentative
⊦	A bluffer
P	Direct
⎮	Inhibited
⍴	Persistent
⍴	Positive
⎮⎮	Restless
P	Sensual
⊦	Slightly argumentative
⊐	Uninhibited
⊦⊦	Very argumentative
⊦	Yielding

Q

	⍴	Aggressive/assertive
	⎧	A bluffer
⎧	⍴	Desire for change
	Q	Direct
	⍴	Inhibited
⎧	⎧	Persistent
	⍴	Sensual
	⍴	Uninhibited

R

	⋏	Creative
	⋏	Cultured
⋎	R	Direct
	⋏	Fatalistic
	ℓ	Inhibited
	⋌	Needle-sharp mind
	⋋	Nervous
	⋏	Relentless
	⋏ℓ	Sings out loud
	⋏	Sings to self
	⋏	Sings to self and others
	⋎	Tenacious
⋏	R	Uninhibited

S

~~D~~ Desire for attention

S Direct/simplicity

𝒮h Fluidity

𝒞S Greedy

~~S~~ Inhibited

⌒ Pushover

𝘚 ⋏ Sensual

𝘚 S Uninhibited

T

⊤ 𝑡 Acquisitive

𝑡 Arrogant

𝑡 Bossy

∪ Careless/forgetful

𝐿 Cautious

𝑡 Conceited

⊤ ⊔ Daydreamer

𝑡 Decisive

⊤ Direct

↑ Disciplined

𝑡 Dominant

⋏ Drug abuser

𝑡 Enthusiastic

𝑡 Ethical

⊤ 𝑡 Fickle/irresponsible

th th Fluid

⊤ High goals

𝖚 Impatient

⊔ Impractical

𝑡 Indecisive

𝑡 Independent

⊤ Jealous

⊤t Leisurely

𝑡 Low goals

𝑡 Optimistic

𝑏 Perfectionistic

𝑡 Persistent

𝖚𝑡 Positive

𝑡 Practical goals

−∪ Procrastination

𝑡 Proud

✗ Reserved

𝑡 Sarcastic

𝓑 Self-castigating

𝑡 Self-conscious

𝒳 Self-controlled

𝑡 Sensitive to
criticism

𝒌 Sensual

⊤ Strong-willed

✗ ⅄ Stubborn

∝ Supersensitive/ exaggerated

ℓ Temper

ℓ Tenacious

↳ Underestimation of self

ℓ Vain

ℓ Weak willed

U

ʎ Acquisitive

U— Cautious

U U Direct

UL Drug abuser

U Jealous

ʎ Matter-of-fact

U Self-deceitful

U Sensual

V

∪ Accumulative

∨ Analytical

∨ Direct

⅄ Keen, sharp-minded

↘ Shy/reserved

‿ Superficial

∨ Uninhibited

W

W Analytical

ʍ Diplomatic

W Direct

ᗡW Envious

ᘈ Fatalistic

ʍ Hesitant

⌤W Humorous

ᗝW Jealous

ᴜⱳ ᴄⱳ Possessive

ʍ ʍ Resentful

ⱳ Self-conscious

ⱳ Worried

X

)(X Aloof

X Direct

X Perfectionistic

X Temper

Y

y Acquisitive

Υ Analytical

y A bluffer

y Clannish

y y Denial of sexual pleasures

y y Determined

Y Direct

y Exaggerated sex drive

y Fatalistic

yl Fluid

y Hesitant

y y Introspective

y Irresponsible

y Jealous

y Keen, sharp-minded

y Loner

y The Night Nurse

y Nonverbal mover

y Only interested in the chase

y Positive

uy uy Possessive

y y Rejection

y Relentless

y Resentful

y y Restless

y Selective

ÿ Self-conscious

y Selfish

y y Sexual aggression

y Sexually vain

y The Stroker

y y Tenacious

y y Wants sex four times a day

y Worried

Z

z Aggressive

3 Clannish

z Confused

Ζ Direct

Ζ Egotistical

z Z Intense concentration

Ζ Lack of attention

Z Moderate

z Perfectionistic

z Sensual

MISCELLANEOUS

look Concentration

flows Confused

nine Immature

intuitive Intuitive

look No attention span

Acknowledgments

THEY SAY IT takes a village to raise a child—well, for me it took the entire world from Cambridge, England, to California, from Baton Rouge to Brixton, England, and then some, to prepare this book. There are so many people to whom I am indebted. My heartfelt thanks go to:

My ancestors, for paving the way so I could be free. Their spirits continue to guide and inspire me.

All the participants who generously allowed me to use their handwriting samples. Without them there would be no book.

All five hundred men I interviewed, for their time and candor.

Every working mother is faced with child-care issues. I have been fortunate to have these wonderful women, who have loved and cared for my son and left me no time to worry: Jenny French, Mrs. Powers, Mrs. Barnes, and Mrs. Baker, and also my son's grandmas, Mrs. Jett and Mrs. East.

Ness Shirley of PACE, for introducing the science to me, and for her constant support and encouragement.

Tony Fairweather of the Write Thing, London, for his vision when I first suggested the idea for the book, and for sending me back to the drawing board when he saw the first draft.

My editor, Manie Barron, and my literary agents, Wanda Akin and Carol Randolph, for making it happen.

Jeanne Roush of Personnel Profiles, my other graphological eye, for patiently checking and rechecking samples for me.

Hedi Butler—when there were no words to write, I was inspired by you.

Carolyn Dukes Alexander, for her poems and our Saturday morning "power talks."

Colin Channer, Bebe Moore Campbell, and Patrice Gaines, for their generosity in endorsing this book and guiding me through the process.

First Class, Inc., in Washington, D.C., for providing a platform for making this book into a workshop.

Faye Williams and Cassandra Burton of Sisterspace & Books, my second home and host store.

D. Muhsinah Berry-Dawan, for her spiritual wisdom and encouragement when I faded.

Becky Singleton, for keeping me in shape.

Dr. Ralph Demmick, for his patience and lending me his brilliant mind.

Before I was ever qualified in anything, my lifelong friends Imani Abdullah Muhameed, Doreen Chambers, Maureen Bryan, Angela Wynter, Karen Merritt, and Rosita Holsey-Stevens were instrumental in my growth and development.

In memory of my dearest Yvonne Toppin—I miss her laughter and the wonderful times we shared together.

A special thank-you to my "J" sisters: Jay Byrd (my blood sister), Jennifer Allen (my niece), Jean Tomlin Russell, Jane Rollands, Janet Burton, Joy Goode, Joanne Simmons, Joleta Douglas, Jackee Holder, Jacquie Moses Roden, Jacqueline Hughes Mooney, and Pasha Kincaid (formerly known as Jacqui).

To all my brother friends: I would get in too much trouble if I mentioned all of you, but special love goes out to Frank Russell, Frankie Bryan, Trevor Coley, and Clifton Culpepper.

Chris Loeffler of Mind and Virginia DeLeo of Character Profiles, for sharing their samples.

Peter Collard, for his flexibility.

Barbara Vance, Brenda Emmanus, Brenda Golden, Lorenda Gordon, Pamela Payton, Carole Pyke, Michele Goode, Yoko Oriyama, Sherain Ely Alemazekoor, Ruth Dutoit, and Claire Nelson.

My D.C. Caribbean Sisters, whose love and support and wonderful lunches have kept me from falling into my "homesick blues": Rosemarie Edwards, Michelle Cross Fenty, Jennifer Loud, Lizette Felix, Donna Coley Trice, Arlene Graham, Tasha Stewart, and Louise Klees Wallace.

Natalie Bridgewater, for jumping in at the last minute when I needed help on the manuscript.

Violetta Anderson and Helen McGlyn. Every girl needs bankers that can perform miracles.

All my friends and family in London, Jamaica, and the United States, for their love and constant support.

My spiritual teachers, who have helped me redirect my life through their wisdom: Patricia Agana, Moyo Francis, and Iylana Vanzant.

All my Strokes & Slants clients and volunteers.

The crew of the AAWOT and the Inner Visions team.

Anita Williams, Renee Nash, and the WHUR family.

Maria Morris and Kay Duda and the Arbour Office staff.

Erica Sheppard, who is on death row and who keeps my life in perspective.

Last but not least, my supportive and patient husband, David, who makes everything possible, and my flexible, adorable son, Diag, who makes mothering not only a privilege and a joy but also a piece of cake.

It is an honor to have each and every one of you in my life and I appreciate all you have given me.

BEVERLEY EAST, a master graphologist, is a leading authority on handwriting. She is a founding member of the Association of Qualified Graphologists. She also identifies forged documents and signatures for private investigators and attorneys. She has been a frequent guest on TV and radio, and has been interviewed by *Emerge, Heart and Soul, The Washington Post, Golf Digest, Pen World,* and *Woman's World,* and has participated in African-American Women on Tour conferences in America and International Women's Week empowerment seminars in England. The client list for her consulting firm, Strokes & Slants, includes the Washington Court Hotel in America and the Queen Elizabeth Foundation for Disabled People and the Write Thing in London. She lives in Washington, D.C., and London with her husband and son. Her website is www.writeanalysis.com.